Broken, Broke and Brought Back

Keith Gilliam

Broken, Broke and Brought Back
© 2020 by Keith Gilliam

Unless otherwise noted, all Scripture quotations in this material are taken from the Holy Bible *English Standard Version* (ESV), Copyright © 2001 by Crossway, a publishing ministry of Good News Publishers. Used by permission. All rights reserved. Other versions used include: Holy Bible, *New International Version* (NIV), Copyright © 1973, 1978, 1984 by Zondervan. Used by permission. All rights reserved. Holy Bible, *New Living Translation* (NLT), Copyright © 1996, 2004, 2015 by Tyndale House Foundation. Used by permission. All rights reserved. Holy Bible, *New King James Version*, Copyright © 1982, Thomas Nelson Publishers. Used by permission. All rights reserved. Holy Bible, *The Message*, Copyright © 2002, Eugene H. Peterson, Published by NavPress. Used by permission. All rights reserved. Holy Bible, *Berean Study Bible* (BSB), Copyright © 2016, Bible Hub. Used by permission. All rights reserved. And the Holy Bible, *King James Version* (KJV).

DEDICATION

To my forever loving, forgiving, faithful wife, Rana, whom God gave me in my youth to serve as a vessel of grace in my wandering manhood.

And to my daughters, Kasey and Briley, whom I admire for their wisdom, discernment, and ability to forgive.

And to my granddaughters, whose eyes I look upon with wonder and awe at the dreams and realities that lie before you.

And most of all to Jesus Christ for offering salvation and forgiveness as a free gift, Who has directed and is directing my path to this day. Where would I be without Your love.

CONTENTS

Broken, Broke and Brought Back

ACKNOWLEDGMENTS

I want to thank the following for their lasting friendship and countless hours of professional proofreading of this book:

Mrs. Tammie Burger, Christian vocalist, teacher, principal and friend.

Dr. Cheryl McAuley, Christian, author, Army veteran and friend.

Forward

I have known Keith Gilliam for most of my life. In fact, Keith has had a profound impact on my relationship with Jesus Christ. I have always appreciated his spiritual insight and believe you will as well. In this work, he has done a marvelous job of capturing the value of "one decision". If reading this book could help you avoid catastrophic sin in your life and help you grow closer to Christ would it be worth reading? I believe that if these thought provoking words are taken to heart it can do just that. This work will take you on a journey from brokenness to redemption, that will leave you thinking about the impact of your "next decision" for the rest of your life. Read this book, pray over its words, and your life will be better for it!

Wendell Brown
Founder - Tragedy Into Triumph
District Superintendent Church of the Nazarene

Preface

"He must increase, but I must decrease" – John 3:30

The mark of a person who is spiritually bankrupt is giftedness without service, knowledge without wisdom, ministry without love and life without purpose.

We are all just one decision away from losing everything, resulting in complete bankruptcy of emotions, relationships, even money and material possessions. One bad decision can ruin a reputation and rob your joy and peace. One decision can turn your life around and point it in a completely different direction all together. One decision could cost you everything you hold dear, including financial security, family and future. One decision.

We all stand at the threshold of decisions every moment of every day that could derail our lives, if acted upon, could cause unparalleled heartache and damage even for the most innocent in our lives. It happened to me.

Though our sinful flesh may get away with a few instances of bad behavior (maybe even many instances), the Bible is clear – your sins will surely find you out (Numbers 32:23). It is not the devil that causes us to sin, but he certainly is seeking someone to destroy.

Peter's warning is a warning for us all: *"Be sober-minded; be watchful. Your adversary the devil prowls around like a roaring lion, seeking someone to devour. Resist him, firm in your faith, knowing that the same kinds of suffering are being experienced by your brotherhood throughout the world"* (1 Peter 5:8-9).

For me, one decision became another decision because it was such a well-kept secret, at least I thought it was. Once a line is crossed, it seems impossible to go back – a new course is charted, a new blueprint is drawn. Sure, you may be able to dabble with sin a time or two and turn from it, but the allure of sin calls us back, again and again, until we are exposed by the light of God's grace, and then, the damage is done, it's too late. Or is it?

God's grace finds us all as sinners with our only hope being God's sovereign work of sending His only Son, Jesus, to die for our sins. So, in reality, we are all at one time one decision away from committing our lives to Christ in complete devotion; and when we make that decision, His love abounds in our hearts, minds and souls. We see life from a new perspective with a new purpose than before. Then, we really do have a new course charted and a new blueprint begins to be drawn.

Sadly, a committed life does not always stay that way. Rare is the man who runs wide open from his values, more likely is the man who drifts ever so slowly from them over a period of time, with small, seemingly insignificant decisions, finding himself in a place he never intended. The offering of our bodies as living sacrifices (Romans 12:1) presents the possibility that living sacrifices are capable of removing themselves from the altar on which they were placed, and turning back from the loving embrace of a heavenly Father, Who, has promised He will never turn His back on us (Hebrews 13:5).

The enemy of God is like a seductress, ever presenting himself in forms that appeal most to our carnal nature, but never providing the promises he produced. God's enemy is the devil, and his promises are always lies, that is what he does, that is his character; he can do nothing else but lie, and his lies are designed to steal, kill and destroy (John 10:10). He will lie to you, he will lie about you, and he will tempt you to lie on his behalf. Any lie honors the devil and dishonors God; only truth honors God.

As I reveal my story in the following pages, please understand I am not a victim of any conspiracy, collusion or coercion by man. My decisions were mine to make, and I made them by my own volition. There is no one for me to blame but myself. Opportunities for escape were afforded me, but my selfish desires gave way to my own dreadful decisions. God always provides a way out (1 Corinthians 10:13), but sadly we often foolishly look the other way. That is what I did.

Bear in mind I will not share names or specifics about my transgression. Ephesians 5 speaks of sexual sin and says, *"it is shameful even to speak of the things that they do in secret. But when anything is exposed by the light, it becomes visible."* (Ephesians 5:12-13) Since my sin was exposed by the light of God's grace, it is visible, but it would be shameful to share details. But it is the grace of God for which I am most thankful and that will in reality, but the only hope for anyone caught in sin and seeking to be restored to wholeness.

While nearly everyone would agree that God's grace is available for anyone who falls, there are some who will claim that a fallen pastor should never be restored to the pulpit. My opinion and my experience is that a pastor who has sinned can in fact be restored to pastoral ministry, provided the way back is biblical, including the trusted council of godly people, and, of course being removed from leadership and preaching ministry for a season.

What you will find in the pages that follow is my story, weaved together with warnings and advice for others who may find themselves in a fallen state, or, even an extended period of turbulent temptation. While I make no guarantees what you will read will force change in your own mind, soul and spirit, I can say that God has afforded me this platform to serve as a witness of a man who had a solid life, ministry and marriage, exchanging it for the devil's lies. I brazenly blazed my own path, breaching trust and finding brokenness; but God brought me back.

It is my sincere prayer God will allow you time to read and then mediate on what you read. My hope is you will not rush through these pages but will pause along the way to pray for God's presence and His delivery. It is my prayer you will find the strength to seek the counsel of a trusted, godly friend or two who will be a source of accountability and assurance.

Statistics prove far too many pastors are falling from the prideful decisions they make. If this book can be of help to just one, then it has been worth my time to write, and I pray you will find it worth your time to read.

For Him,
Keith Gilliam
John 3:30 <>

Introduction

Labels

"When men speak ill of thee, live so as nobody may believe them." – Plato

U.S. companies spent 223 billion dollars on marketing in 2019 [1] – all in an effort to persuade as many people as possible to buy their products and services that we may or may not want or even need. And it works. A glance at nearly any label will tell a lot about the product because of the advertising dollars spent to influence perception.

Advertisers are masters at creating images and jingles that we may find ourselves thinking about or even humming long after we have viewed or heard the advertisement. Product brands are created to be so easily recognizable that some companies now have wordless logos with no words at all accompanying the logo and we still recognize the brand simply by the brand mark.

Consider *Nike, Starbucks, Target, Pepsi, Apple, Dominos,* and *McDonalds* to name a few. Even *Major League Baseball* and *MasterCard* have wordless logos. The mere mention of those companies will produce an image in your mind; and the mind will produce a thought, and perhaps a desire, followed by what each company hopes is a purchase.

Then there are the catchy little wordless jingles with just a few notes that are instantly identifiable when heard. If you read, *"Intel inside,"* you can likely hear the four note jingle. That *"bong"* as it is called was composed more than 20 years ago and some estimate that it may be played over one million times a day around the world. [2]

How about the five note *McDonald's* jingle, "Ba da ba ba ba," before their very familiar, "I'm lovin' it" slogan. *(I'm betting you just hummed that tune in your head.)*

It takes less than three seconds to hear the AT&T four note theme.

Those mental snapshots and sounds become planted in

our subconscious and will resurface occasionally, sometimes with very little or no prompting. Our minds are powerful enough to keep those images without us even attempting to store them. Sometimes I wake in the morning with a song on my mind with no idea how it got there; it has been buried in my subconscious and resurfaces when I wake. The mind is a powerful tool, storing thoughts and image for future retrieval.

The art of creating recognizable images and phrases in the mind is called labeling, and it works quite well for major advertisers at causing us to remember and prompting us to buy whatever the seller is attempting to sell. Advertisers seek to saturate your thoughts with their products that you will think of them without even a conscious effort to think of them.

While reading the list of advertisers I included above, you no doubt had some mental images roll through your mind and you may have even found that you are hungry even at the mention of *McDonalds*, *Starbucks*, *Pepsi* or *Dominos*.

While labeling may be a great tool for advertisers, labeling is not the way we are supposed to treat and think about people, especially as Christians. And yet, we all live with labels, images or jingles that will cause us to create a snapshot of a person and condense what we see or know about them into a word or small phrase. And sometimes we think of someone without even trying to think of them. Have you ever had someone "just cross your mind" and you did not know why? And with the thought of that person comes a label, an identifier that we have placed on them because of our past experiences or their past behavior.

We are all likely guilty of labeling people based on a myriad of things: income, race, weight, religion, piercings and tattoos, education, denominational affiliation, vocation, fashion and dress; and the list could go on. Even though we have been warned since we were children to resist the urge, we really do judge books by covers and reducing what we see in others to a single sentence or an antidote, an image or a jingle, a four note "bong," if you will.

One of my favorite labels has to do with church denominations. By "favorite," I do not mean that I enjoy the label, I mean that it is a favorite to discuss. Church labeling is actually a great frustration of mine and those labels can be very destructive to the body of Chsit.

18

When someone tells you they are Catholic, for example, you likely have a set of preconceived ideas that you immediately superimpose on that person because of your knowledge or image of Catholicism. The same is true with any denomination, Baptist, Methodist, Anglican, Pentecostal, Lutheran, Episcopalian, Nazarene, Catholic; and the list goes on. There are likely already labels planted in your mind regarding any denomination and probably certain labels if you hear of a non-denominational church.

When asked by people what "kind" of church I pastor, I know they want to know the denominational affiliation, but I will generally simply answer with "a Christian church," because I want to avoid the stereotypes they may form if I tell them anything else. Unfortunately, even withholding that information can create a label of its own in the mind of some, and, the word "Christian" has become a label in and of itself.

Too often, with a quick glance, we have created a virtual summary based on what we see, hear and imagine built on past experiences, hearsay, or preconceived notions. Like product labels we do not even need any words in order to judge, just the very presence of the image of someone's countenance, clothing or conduct will be enough for us to hear the jingle and recognize the "bong."

Labeling – we all do it: and if you are guilty of labeling others, then it stands to reason that others are guilty of labeling you. And the fear of being labeled can create tension and stress in one's life, often times paralyzing those who are not willing to gain control of their own fear.

When you fear being labelled, you could spend an inordinate amount of time worrying about how people feel and what they think of you, your behavior and even your choices and decisions. That fear can control your behavior, spending habits, financial decisions, even the friends you choose and where you shop.

Many years ago, as a young youth pastor in large churches I found it was impossible to keep everyone happy, try as I may; teenagers and parents alike; not to mention the senior pastor and other staff members, and even volunteers. Everyone had a varying opinion about the purpose and direction the youth ministry should take. No matter what I did it seemed someone was going to be disappointed, frustrated or even angry (*"righteously indignant"* for the Christian).

That was a tough place to be as a young man who selfishly wanted everyone to like me and for everyone to be happy with my leadership. I found that it is impossible to make everyone happy, and yet I did not want to be labeled by anyone based on a decision I made that they did not like or agree with. The fear of being labeled nearly paralyzed my ability to make decisions and lead effectively.

It was my father-in-law's godly counsel that caused me to re-think my philosophy when he told me, "If you are making everyone happy, you are doing something wrong." That was his way of saying, "You cannot make everyone happy, and you are wasting your time trying."

I realized he was right and that I needed to chart a new course, to draw a new blueprint for my life and my leadership. But the idea that people could be unhappy and talking about me when I was not around nagged me. Until I began to pray that God's Holy Spirit would be my witness even when I was not present to defend myself. That was liberating.

I did not believe that suddenly everyone would think

highly of me no matter what they heard; that my labels would disappear; rather, I was becoming free to be myself the way God created me without the bondage of fear that others may not like me or my decisions.

While many consider the antithesis of love to be hate, I believe that fear opposes love.

Paul wrote to Timothy about the issue of fear when he penned these words, *"God gave us a spirit not of fear but of power and love and self-control"* (2 Timothy 1:7).

I notice two important truths from that verse:

First, a *"spirit of fear"* exists – it paralyzes people every day, even Christ followers.

But second, and this is really important, it is **not** a spirit that comes from God.

One of the greatest concerns I have for the modern-day church is the existence of fear among her members. Fear can literally paralyze people from making godly decisions and fear can drive wedges of distrust between members. Fear is a tool of the devil. Fear must be recognized as the product of God's enemy and not God Himself. God is not the Father of fear, God is the Father of power, love and a sound mind (or self-discipline).

God's Word says, *"There is no fear in love, but perfect love casts out fear. For fear has to do with punishment, and whoever fears has not been perfected in love"* (1 John 4:18).

I am a pretty simple man, but it stands to reason that if God cannot please everybody, what should cause me to think I can? The answer is: fear.

Everyone does not even agree that God exists, and yet His power is unmistakable for those who believe. So, it is best for you to realize, "You cannot make everyone happy, and you are wasting your time trying."

It was Plato who said, *"The untrained mind keeps up a running commentary, labelling everything, judging everything. Best to ignore that commentary. Don't argue or resist, just ignore. Deprived of attention and interest, this voice gets quieter and quieter and eventually just shuts up."*

I am not sure that I completely agree with Plato that it "eventually just shuts up." Depriving our imagination of those labels becomes almost a never ending endeavor, it never seems to just shut up. But that voice can get quieter and quieter the more we shift the focus of our attentions and affections away from ungodly, unholy things, resisting the man-made labels that seem to attach themselves to us.

The wisdom of God as spoken through the Apostle Paul warrants our attention here. Near the end of his epistle to the saints in Philippi, Paul gives this caution; *"Summing it all up, friends, I'd say you'll do best by filling your minds and meditating on things true, noble, reputable, authentic, compelling, gracious—the best, not the worst; the beautiful, not the ugly; things to praise, not things to curse"* (Philippians 4:8 TM).

Let's face it, you hear yourself talk more than anyone else through what is called "self-talk." No matter how much your spouse, children, co-workers or boss talks to you, no one talks to you more than you talk to you. Again, the mind is powerful and if we consistently listen to the voice we hear telling us we are worthless, unloved and unlovable we will be tempted to come to believe it.

Best to train your mind to ignore that commentary and train your mind to think on the best, not the worst. Best to think on the things God instructs rather than the things that self-instructs. The things God instructs can construct; the things that self-instructs can destruct.

Think on the things of God and He will construct a positive image in you of how He sees you. Think on the things that self-instructs and you will see how destructive you can be to yourself, and others.

The reality is, we are not only tempted to buy the labels that others place on us, but we can even be guilty of placing labels on ourselves, led by negative self-talk when we hear the awful things the enemy wants us to hear about ourselves.

If we are ever brave enough to peer behind the labels we generate we will generally find that other people are a lot like us, and that can be difficult for us to admit.

We are all simultaneously alike and unique. Fear elevates the differences and ignores the similarities. Fear breeds unhealthy competition. Fear paralyzes and conjures up the worst possible images.

Power, love and self-discipline, on the other hand, awards others for their accomplishments and is not jealous when others win or receive accolades that we perhaps desire for ourselves.

This is the point of 1 Corinthians 13 when Paul offers us a list of the attributes of love. Patient, not envious. Kind, not rude. Selfless, not arrogant.

We are all very similar. We have similar fears and fantasies; similar desires and dreams; similar interests and intents.

But the one thing we certainly all share in common is ***temptation***.

I once knew a woman who claimed she was above temptation; *"I cannot be tempted,"* she boasted. And yet the Bible tells us a different story; the Bible tells the Truth. Not one of us is exempt from temptation. Jesus Himself was tempted in every way as we, yet He did not sin (Hebrews 4:15). Jesus was fully God, yet fully man. You and I are mere mortals created in the image of God and yet born with a sin nature that is persistently bent toward pleasing self no matter the cost to others. We are all prone to temptation, and we will never escape that temptation while on this side of heaven.

So, let's stop pretending that you are above temptation, especially the temptation to label others. Let's stop pretending that you are not "label-able" by someone in some way, on any given day. Whatever we do or avoid will cause people to label us. No matter what you do or refuse to do brings the ability for someone to place a label on you, whether you feel it is justified or not. And if you are not careful, you will grow to fear those labels which can have crippling, devastating effects on you and your ministry.

Richard Dortch was a nationally known TV host and associated with Jim Bakker and Heritage USA for those of you old enough to remember the shakedown in the 1980's. Dortch was indicted in 1989 of conspiracy and wire and mail fraud where he was sentenced to prison. He was labeled a convicted felon, despite all the work of the Lord accomplished around the world through the PTL Ministries. [3]

I'm sure that I have had my share of labels placed on me over the years, some I was aware of, and others I'm clueless to. But, since my teenage conversion to Christ, my deepest, growing desire has been to be known as a devoted Christ follower – I have grown into that belief, it did not just happen. I do not live in the allusion that I have reached a level of earthly perfection like some seem to believe and am incapable of sinning.

I am both a saint of God because of His work of grace in my life, and a sinner who is hopeless without the amazing grace of God. I am still a sinner; I still sin occasionally and am tempted to sin often. I still occasionally have thoughts that are not godly. Sometimes I allow anger to rise up and create a chasm between me and my wife. Sometimes I am tempted to join in the gossip train as it whistles by when others are aboard telling tales of other people. The tendency to that behavior is a natural human condition, but it is a condition that God wants us to fight off and steer clear of. The Apostle Paul said,

"Let all bitterness and wrath and anger and clamor and slander be put away from you, along with all malice." [4]

As Christ followers, our battles are always won in prayer.

I love the story in 1 Samuel of the Philistines capturing the Ark of the Covenant. Israel was defeated, lost about 4,000 men in the battle, and lost the Ark to the Philistines. When Israel dared do battle with the Philistines again to attempt to retake the Ark, the Philistines were ready and defeated them again. Though the Philistines were afraid (1 Samuel 4:7), they were convinced that they could defeat the throws of their enemy, Israel. One verse stands out to me; *"Take courage, and be men, O Philistines, lest you become slaves to the Hebrews as they have been to you; **be men and fight**"* (1 Samuel 4:9 **emphasis mine**).

Often times we give people many reasons to label us because we simply are not willing to, *"Fight the good fight of the faith"[5]*. Rather than being men and fighting, we often times surrender to the war waging within us.

Romans warns us, *"I delight in the law of God, in my inner being, but I see in my members another law waging war against the law of my mind and making me captive to the law of sin that dwells in my members"* (Romans 7:22-23).

Again, as Christ followers, our battles are always won in prayer. When we *"fight like men,"* we do so in the posture of prayer.

Yes, sadly we often times give people plenty of reasons to label us. The Good News is, however, God has already labeled us worthy by sending His Son to die for us.

Statistically, plenty of people, even Christians in our

society do not have, what I would call, a healthy world view based on the teachings of Scripture. Perhaps it is better said that most people, including many Christians, have a world view that does not line up with the Scriptural perspective of how life is supposed to be lived. The statistics are staggering:

- Up to 25 percent of married men and 11 percent of married women will cheat at some point in their lives, [6]

- As many as 59% of Millennials believe pornography is morally acceptable.

- Forty percent of pastors surveyed admitted to having an extra marital affair after entering the ministry.

And yet God's Word is clear that adultery is a sin. Nevertheless, if you fall to the sin of adultery, you will be labeled.

My moral failure while pastoring a church was a horrific experience for the entire local body of believers. But what hurt most was what one Sunday school teacher had to tell one of her young students about my departure. *"Pastor Keith broke a commandment."*

There it was. I was labeled. An adulterer. A breaker of

the Ten Commandments.

If you have committed any egregious sin, especially if it was a sin that garnered a great deal of public attention, like it or not, you have been labeled. No matter what accomplishments or successes you had before, they will all pale in comparison to the label you will have following a horrific public transgression.

Bill Hybels founded Willow Creek Community Church in South Barrington, Illinois in 1975 with a handful of friends. The church grew quickly and eventually became recognized as a strong outreach church with a global emphasis for ministry. Once considered the largest church in America, the church was not without internal controversy. As Bill prepared to retire in 2018, accusations surfaced that he had committed adultery with a married woman and had acted inappropriately with another woman on his staff years before. Needless to say, that accusation tarnished his 40 years of vibrant, public ministry. Sexual sin labels can be devastating and can obviously ruin relationships and reputations.

Being labeled by sin does not have to be the end. There is hope for us all to come back and start anew. Sexual sin does not have to be the end of the road for anyone, including pastors and those serving the church, any more than any other sin should not be the end. We serve a God of second chances who does not toss us aside when we fail, rather, He surrounds us with His grace and even His discipline to lovingly bring us back to wholeness and holiness, if we are willing to accept His loving discipline and humbly receive His amazing grace. God only uses sinners to accomplish His will, because that's all He has to work with.

Consider David, who is remembered as *"a man after God's own heart"* (see 1 Samuel 13:14; Acts 13:22), yet he committed adultery *and* murder (2 Samuel 11).

My wife and I have had the privilege of speaking at a number of marriage events. We often share that it has been our experience that adultery is not only grounds for divorce, it can also be grounds for forgiveness and reconciliation, that's what happened for us. While that will take a period of time, patience, prayer, and perhaps a great deal of counseling, it is possible to regain trust and have hope for a bright future again – your heart and your passion for God can be renewed. Reconciliation requires effort and commitment from both parties; the offended, and the offender, but it can be done.

So, how about you? Have you faced temptation and fallen? Do you find it difficult to resist the constant barrage of thoughts of lusts? More importantly, do you want to be remembered as "a man after God's own heart"?

Then I invite you to read on.

Broken, Broke and Brought Back

Chapter 1

Reconcile

*"Integrity is telling myself the truth. And honesty is
telling the truth to other people."*
– Spencer Johnson

The Compass of Compassion

Navigating the open seas with no compass would be a
veritable suicide mission. If you don't know where you
are going, then any path will do, and could lead to a
great deal of drifting and wandering, and even pain.
Without a compass we are hopelessly lost, committing to
rely on only chance to bring us what we think we need
and take us where we think we need to go.

It is interesting to me that the word *compassion* begins
with the word *compass*. If it is a compass that helps us
define true north, then it is compassion that helps us
define true love. We never really know love until we

give it away, so we must have a compass in our compassion in order to judge correctly that we are going in the right direction.

My wife and I recently welcomed our fifth granddaughter into the world. Just when I thought I could not love another like I have loved the ones before, God has expanded my heart and made more room. Very typical of God, since He has no limit to His love for us, or the number of people who continue to come to Him. I know how to love, not because of loving my wife for 40 years, or my two adult daughters, or my other four granddaughters; I know how to love because of the compass, the direction of God's love toward me.

It is God Himself that gives us the very ability to even know what love is and how to exercise love.

1 John 4:19, *"We love because he first loved us."*

Consider where we would be if it were not for God, Who loved us even while we were yet sinners, He sent His Son to die for us (Romans 5:8).

Hiking in the dark without a compass could find you walking in circles.

Living without compassion can find you walking in darkness.

It seems that people are almost magnetically drawn to people who are truly compassionate and love without condition. Those who have fixed their eyes on Jesus and recognize that love can breach any barrier are people that others tend to be drawn to. The challenge is for us to follow the Compass of God, His Son, and allow Him to lead us to places where lost and hurting people are. And, to recognize that God loves us with such abandon that we can do nothing to cause Him to ever hate us or abandon us.

Integrity

Courtrooms are sacred places in our society. When a judge sets rules for the courtroom, he or she expects that everyone will follow them. In 2013 Michigan's Chief District Judge Raymond Voet, fined himself $25 when his own phone went off during the prosecutor's closing arguments – a rule that he himself had put in place. He admitted, "I broke the rule and I have to live by it." [7] Many would say that Judge Voet is a man of integrity because of his willingness to fine himself in his own courtroom when he broke his own rule.

Honesty & Truth

The truth is a heavy burden that few care to carry it.
– Jewish Proverb

People have long confused the meaning of the word's *honesty* and *truth*, using them synonymously as if each has the same meaning. It is no wonder that we have mistaken the similarity – nearly any dictionary or thesaurus will provide both words as interchangeable.

But how can we know the difference and what difference does it even make? In other words, is there a distinction between the meaning of the words, *honesty* and *truth*?

Most often, people will define integrity as being honest; nothing related to truth, because we see honesty and truth as one and the same. But the two are different.

Simply put, honesty has to do with one's feelings and opinions, while truth deals with accurate representations of reality. Honesty may be subjective, while truth is objective.

Someone may claim to be honest with you; however, their *honesty* is based on their own feelings or opinions which may or may not represent reality, or truth. We see the world through the prism we see it through and oft times that prism is skewed due to our environment, past or influence of others.

In politics we find some great examples. In a two-party system such as we have in our country, either party can take any cause and claim that they are being honest, while failing to recognize *the truth*. Some politicians will even use truth and honesty synonymously.

To my knowledge no one has ever been asked in a court proceeding to "Swear to be honest, completely honest, nothing but honest." The typical swearing in calls for witnesses to "Swear to tell the truth, the whole truth and nothing but the truth." How one believes may be honestly wrong, completely devoid of truth.

Jesus words were controversial 2,000 years ago and remain controversial today, *"I am the way, and the truth, and the life. No one comes to the Father except through me"* (John 14:6).

Notice that Jesus did not claim to be honest, though I'm sure He always was. His claim is the representation of the reality that He is the One and Only Son of the One True God. *Honesty* portrays our feelings or opinions, truth represents reality. *Truth* remains truth regardless of who if anyone believes.

Jesus is the truth – not everyone believes that reality, but His statement is truth because He is truth. Jesus is not truth because I believe it; I believe it because it is true.

In John 8 Jesus said, *"If you abide in my word, you are truly my disciples, and you will know the truth, and the truth will set you free"* (John 8:31-32).

Jesus' declaration in John 8 is **not** that our honesty will set us free, rather knowing the truth from His Word and abiding in It. *Abide* literally means to remain in it; so, truth is only found in remaining in the Word of God in relationship with Jesus Christ, Who is the very essence of truth. Any deviation from the Word of God sets one up on a path that's ultimate destination is destruction.

Though we often use the words *honesty* and *truth* interchangeably, they are not synonymous. It seems that our society has developed its own standard for honesty, while leaving objective truth behind.

Allow me to illustrate.

With so many varying philosophies on virtually any

subject imaginable, people can embrace an ideal and honestly believe what they have been told or have discovered on their own, but it may be devoid of truth. A small child may honestly believe that Santa Claus or the Easter bunny are real, only to discover the truth of the mythical characters in later years.

Truth, on the other hand, stands in direct opposition to many of the beliefs that so many people accept and *honestly* believe. Jesus, again, never claimed to be honest, although I believe He was honest; He declared, however, that He is the Truth.

It is vitally important to understand the difference between honesty and truth in light of integrity as we move into the subject of reconciliation. As we will soon discover, many people, even well-meaning clergy, accept the lies of God's enemy as truth and move forward as if those lies are reality.

To be reconciled requires both honesty and truth – the sharing of one's perspectives and feelings and acknowledging the truth that may lie from outside us. It is an issue of integrity at the highest calling.

Proverbs says, *"The integrity of the upright guides them,*

but the crookedness of the treacherous destroys them" (Proverbs 11:3).

In order to be reconciled one to another, we must know the difference between honesty and truth, employing both, in order to seek true, biblical integrity. Some may convince themselves that they are being honest because they have persuaded themselves to believe something to be true that frankly is not true.

The word reconcile is a compound word that has Old French and Latin roots; *re* meaning *again*, and *concile* meaning *to make friendly*. So, to reconcile means to *again be friendly*, or, *to bring together again.*

In bookkeeping, reconciliation is the balancing of two accounts so that they are in agreement. To reconcile the books in the financial world is to assure that what is actually being spent matches what is leaving the account.

Too often in marriage there is a lopsided balance sheet of love, giving, compassion and service; one partner is consistently giving more than the other while one partner is left with a deficit of receiving real compassion, love and service. Generally, in a marriage that is out of balance there is a balance sheet that is not reconciling;

one party is taking far too much, and the other party is not receiving enough, so, they are out of balance. *Unreconciled.* This can be true for any relationship, not just marriage.

When financial records are reconciled, an accountant will point out the differences between the two records so that discrepancies can be corrected and the issues that put the books out of balance to begin with will not happen again.

Marriage requires the same kind of accountability, and very often, reconciliation. Couples must be willing to give someone permission to point out the differences to both parties with the intention of gaining a balance and assuring that problems from the past will not linger into the future, all while seeking both honesty *and* truth. Whether a couple has a small group, a professional counselor, or a pastor, giving permission to others to speak into our lives and even our marriages is vital to remaining in balance, or being made friendly again. In fact, it is most helpful to have the wise counsel of many.

Here we find the wisdom of Proverbs, *"Where there is no guidance, a people falls, but in an abundance of counselors there is safety"* (Proverbs 11:14).

Couples who are estranged must be willing *to be made friendly again*, to be brought back together, to be reconciled. If there is an unbalance and one party is not willing to reconcile, there can be no reconciliation.

Frankly, it is sinful when we do not seek and allow the counsel of others in our lives.

Isaiah warns, *"'Woe to the rebellious children,' says the LORD, 'Who take counsel, but not of Me, and who devise plans, but not of My Spirit that they may add sin to sin. Who walk to go down to Egypt, and have not asked for My advice'"* (Isaiah 30:1-2 KJV). While we must be careful the counsel we seek, it is clear that we must involve the godly advice and instruction of others in our lives.

In my case, I did not regularly seek the counsel of others which was a large part of the reason for my fall and subsequent loss of everything. In fact, I was guilty of embezzling from my own spiritual account what God had entrusted to me. My personal emotional account was out of balance and I was too proud to admit it and seek the loving, godly counsel of other men who could have helped me. Pride was my downfall. I was selfishly robbing other men the joy and responsibility of accountability in my life, while I was attempting to provide the very same in the lives of other men.

When you attempt to give what you have not gainfully received in prayer and fellowship with God, you are guilty of a form of embezzling; you are stealing from some other source to pay forward what you do not deserve to pay. That is sin.

So, where do we go wrong when we sin? What is the genesis of our sin? How do we find ourselves in such sinful behavior?

John Eldredge wrote, "You have a say in what your heart gives way to. [The] scriptures [are] urging us to shepherd the life of our heart." [8]

And shepherd it we must – vigilantly.

Too often pastors are guilty of attempting to shepherd the flock God has placed them among while not shepherding their own life or allowing and receiving shepherding from another. Let's face it pastor, you too, are a sheep, in need of a shepherd. You need discipline in order to allow Holy Spirit to guide you, just as your flock does. And if you are reading this and you are not a pastor, you are not exempt. Every one of God's children need this kind of spiritual discipline.

I have known plenty of pastors who study scripture only for sermon preparation and not for the preparation of their own soul. It is the "That'll preach!" mentality of study of scriptures for many pastors. That can be a prideful attitude in need of biblical circumcision of the heart.

The Prophet Jeremiah, *"Circumcise yourselves to the LORD; remove the foreskin of your hearts, O men of Judah and inhabitants of Jerusalem"* (Jeremiah 4:4).

Romans 2 says, *"circumcision is a matter of the heart, by the Spirit, not by the letter"* (Romans 2:29).

In short, we are all in need of someone pointing out the imbalance in our own lives in order to reconcile our life with God and those around us and for our lives to remain reconciled. The issues of the heart can be tricky and must be handled with care and with counsel. But we, like fools, think that our way is right, and we know within ourselves what is best for us without seeking the counsel of the wise (Proverbs 12:15). That is sin!

When we seek our own counsel from within ourselves, we cheapen the act of grace that someone else can have in our life when they provide counsel and correction. Too often we blunder on thinking we have all the knowledge we need, we have it all under control, resting on the grace of God that we believe will keep us no matter what sin we find ourselves in. That is reckless. That is the cheapening of God's grace. That is sin!

Grace is not a license to sin. That is what Dietrich Bonhoeffer called, "cheap grace."[9] Rather, grace is an authorization *not* to sin, but also the ability to come back, as the Prodigal Son, when we wander from our Heavenly Father's loving embrace (see Luke 15:11-32).

Almost every time a person cheapens grace and refuses to allow the accountability we all need; it is due to one of two reasons: thinking too much of ourselves or thinking too little of ourselves. We often have a heightened view of ourselves or a delinquent view of ourselves. We are often guilty of either inflating ourselves by building ourselves up too far or deflating ourselves by not seeing our God-giving value. We must learn to see ourselves as God see us, through the lens of His perfect love.

While some encourage a positive *self-esteem*, I would rather encourage a positive *Christ-esteem*. Instead of esteeming yourself from the perspective of self, it is much more God-honoring to view ourselves as Christ views us.

Michael Courtney suffered several moral failings as a pastor before he found the help he truly needed and eventually turned his life around saving his marriage and winning back the adoration of his children. He wrote a book about his experience in which he wrote, *"The picture we have of ourselves is so contradictory to the way we really are, that we are consumed with shame and guilt over our shortcomings, real or imagined, or we are devastated by feelings of worthlessness and unlovability."*[10]

When my children were little my wife and I would tell them constantly they were each a **wonderful, unique, creation of God**. Like a radio station, we used the call letters WUCG to reiterate the point. It is impossible for God to love us any more than He already does, and it is impossible for Him to love us any less. He loves us with an everlasting love (Jeremiah 31:3). He created us each uniquely in His Own image (Psalm 139:13). We are dearly loved by God. He sees us in ways we do not see ourselves, and He desires that we see ourselves through the lenses of His love and Word *(Christ-esteem)* rather than the lens of our fallen state *(self-esteem)*. While we are tempted to speak death and despair over ourselves, God always speaks life and love over us.

"For we ourselves were once foolish, disobedient, led astray, slaves to various passions and pleasures, passing our days in malice and envy, hated by others and hating one another. But when the goodness and loving kindness of God our Savior appeared, he saved us, not because of works done by us in righteousness, but according to his own mercy, by the washing of regeneration and renewal of the Holy Spirit, whom he poured out on us richly through Jesus Christ our Savior, so that being justified by his grace we might become heirs according to the hope of eternal life" (Titus 3:3-7).

If you have had difficulty with others that have fallen, consider this, you will never look into the eyes of a person that God does not love and cannot forgive; including the person you see in the mirror. You will never look into the eyes of a person who God could love any more than He already does or any less than He already does.

Proverbs says, *"Guard your heart above all else, for it determines the course of your life"* (Proverbs 4:23 NLT).

We are the gatekeepers of our own hearts, to avoid

giving way to temptation. When you surrender to temptation, you are accepting how you view yourself, or how you perceive others view you, over how God views you. More than likely most of you reading this do not see yourselves with the same value God sees you. You may see yourself as a sinful failure, unable to change or to love or even to be loved. Those are the words of our adversary, the devil, straight from the pit of hell. That is precisely why we should *not* be listening to the narrative of our own self-talk, which is too often misguided by the nuances of the enemy.

You have value because God says you have value; you have value because God values you. He has invested Himself in you in the form of His love which He has laid out for you since before the foundation of the world.

Charles Spurgeon preached, *"A material may be almost valueless at first, but when a wise man has exercised his thought and skill upon it, the value may be enhanced a thousand-fold."* [11]

"How precious also are thy thoughts unto me, O God! How great is the sum of them! If I should count them, they are more in number than the sand: when I awake, I am still with thee" (Psalm 139:17).

The unmistakable reality of our sinfulness is that God loves us still. Paul's words to the Corinthians resonate with me here: *"No temptation has overtaken you that is not common to man"* (1 Corinthians 10:13).

Matthew Henry wrote regarding that verse, *"Carnal desires gain strength by indulgence."* [12] Everyone can be and will be tempted, but it is the man who takes his thoughts captive (2 Corinthians 10:5) that wins the battle.

Paul continues his thoughts in 1 Corinthians 10:13 with these words, *"God is faithful, and he will not let you be tempted beyond your ability, but with the temptation he will also provide the way of escape, that you may be able to endure it."*

It has become difficult for men to admit that they are tempted, primarily because we have come to view temptation as a self-inflicted weakness; something that the man enjoys or even invites – brings about at his own invitation, if you will. For example, men who admit that they are tempted to lust, stand the risk of being labeled by others, as if that is the totality of their personality. To make matters worse, we often hear people say things like, "Once a cheat, always a cheat," referring to men who fall into sexual sin, as if God's grace cannot reach the heart of a person who fails or falls.

While we all have sinned and fallen short (Romans 3:23) and we all are tempted to sin, temptation and sin are two different things. James 1:13 says, *"when we are tempted,"* not *"if you are tempted."*

James draws the distinction between temptation and sin: *"Temptation comes from our own desires, which entice us and drag us away. These desires give birth to sinful actions. And when sin is allowed to grow, it gives birth to death."* (James 1:14-16 NLT).

Let's remember that Jesus was *"tempted in every way, just as we are – yet he did not sin"* (Hebrews 4:15 KJV). I dare say that Jesus' temptation was not a result of a self-inflicted weakness, something He chased after. He was fully man; but He was also fully God, incapable of sinning, but capable to serve as a Perfect example of how we are to respond when facing temptation of our own.

I'm convinced that many men when tempted blame themselves for the temptation, beating themselves up emotionally and mentally for the temptation, without even acting on it. But temptation is as natural a part of living as anything we do, recognizing that will go a long way in helping you defeat the constant barrage of temptation that will likely last the rest of your life. We must be sure that we avoid activity that will increase the likelihood of temptation, but the devil is clearly the tempter.

Sin cannot be allowed to be your master when you are under grace. Grace is not a shield we hide our sin behind, rather a banner under which we accept Christ's forgiveness for sins and live toward a sinless existence so as to be pleasing to our Father in Heaven. You may never live a sinless life this side of heaven but that is our aim; scripture tells us:

- *"Awake to righteousness and do not sin"* (1 Corinthians 15:34 NKJV).
- *"... do not let sin reign in your mortal body so that you obey its evil desires."* (Romans 6:12 NIV)

Peter wrote, *"prepare your minds for action; be self-controlled; set your hope fully on the grace to be given you when Jesus Christ is revealed. As obedient children, do not conform to the evil desires you had when you lived in ignorance, but just as he who called you is holy, so be holy in all you do; for it is written, 'Be holy, because I am holy'"* (1 Peter 1:13-16 NIV).

Notice Peter's outline:
- prepare your minds
- be self-controlled
- set your hope fully on the grace

While there have been many authors who offered varying definitions on holiness, allow me to offer my own to frame this discussion: ***Holiness is a life-long journey of 18 inches – from the head to the heart.***

What I mean is, anyone pursing holiness will spend a lifetime convincing their heart of what their head is telling them. And if the mind is constantly speaking the words of the adversary, you'll never understand the true, biblical pursuit of holiness.

Clearly, Paul identify with that sentiment as he proclaimed that he had to *"die daily."* [13]

Biblical holiness is more of a pursuit than a destination. To "die daily" is to keep moving in one's sanctification (spiritual growth) toward a loving, forgiving God, seeking to *"be imitators of God."* (Ephesians 5:1).

Note that Peter starts the holiness process in the mind that is then followed by obedient behavior. Our obedience in those areas is evidenced by our non-conformance to evil desires, and also in our desire to be holy as God is holy. We do not seek a legalistic mindset, only changing our outward behavior and allowing the mind to run free. No. Holiness involves being *"transformed by the renewal of your mind"* (Romans 12:2). What enters the mind is destined for the heart, so Paul's words are appropriate, *"take every thought captive to obey Christ."* [14]

In fact, Peter begins these verses with the word, *"Therefore,"* meaning, he is connecting the preceding thought to the words we just read. Peter opens this letter with the theme of the mercy and hope we have in Jesus Christ. Peter says that we have *"an inheritance that can never perish, spoil or fade."* (1 Peter 1:4)

Imagine you were planning a long trip in which you had to traverse many mountains and valleys, high winds and desert conditions. Taking such a trip would require much preparation. If you were walking, you would no doubt bundle up your clothing so that it would not get caught in the wind or on rocks or tree branches.

I recently helped a friend move across country. Several stops were made to secure the tarp over the items in the bed of the pickup truck. If you are to *"prepare your minds for action,"* you are to *"gird up the loins of your mind"* (1 Peter 1:13), or, batten down the items you plan to take on the trip so that they will survive the journey.

The journey I am speaking of is life. We all live it, and for the genuine Christ follower, we hope that we don't shame the name of Jesus. In order to live a Christ-filled, holy life, we must prepare our minds for the journey as we would prepare our vehicles for a long trip across the country. Your battle for holiness begins in the mind. Cheap grace says, "Hey, since we have a hope that cannot perish, spoil or fade, we may as well live it up!"

> *"True Grace leads to Godly life, a life that seeks after God. A life where our joy and delight are to follow and serve Jesus."* – Ibrahim Emile

Those of us who have experienced true grace are so thankful for the price of our salvation, that we understand grace not as a shield we hide behind, but rather a banner under which we accept the forgiveness offered to us through the death of Jesus Christ. And the gratefulness of His grace drives us to serve and resist temptation, not to go on sinning (Romans 6:1) because we know we are "safe." But when we do sin, we can take heart that we have an Advocate that goes to Father on our behalf (1 John 2:1).

Jesus told his disciples, *"If you love me, you will obey what I command"* (John 14:15 NIV). Keep reading the following verses and you'll find that accomplishing that will not be in our own power, but by *"another Counselor"* the Father will give us – the Spirit of truth. [15]

I am far from faultless and flawless. Even with the presence of God in my life, I, like Paul, have to *"die every day"* (1 Cor. 15:31) to my selfish pride and sin nature that is bent toward self and distance from our Creator. There is a perpetual sense of death in our sanctification (spiritual growth) as we grow into the image of the One Who created us (see 2 Corinthians 3:18).

Paul's letter to the church in Ephesus declares that instead of getting drunk on wine, we should *"be filled with the Holy Spirit."* (Ephesians 5:18). The phrase *"be filled"* literally means *"be being filled"* which is a continual, unending process of becoming like our Master. We must guard our sanctification by whatever means necessary so that we may *"overflow with hope by the power of the Holy Spirit"* (Romans 15:13).

You will never have all of God until He has all of you; and He will never have all of you until you commit to a continual growth pattern of surrender to His grace, beginning with the surrender and transformation of your mind. There is a sense in the spiritual realm that we are already who we are becoming. As Christ followers, we are already sanctified holy and righteous in His eyes, and we are becoming holy and righteous before Him, not because of our behavior, but because of Jesus' sacrifice on the cross. We are becoming who we already are, holy and blameless in His sight (Colossians 1:22).

The soundtrack of my human spirit wants to constantly playback the top ten list of my failures. God's Spirit is constantly beckoning me to change the channel on my human flesh and play His greatest hits over me. The love songs of His Word are personal for each of us.

Jesus did not tell us that we *ought* to be the light of the world, but that we *are* the light of the world (Matthew 5:14). Jesus did not tell us that we *should* be the salt of the earth, but that we *are* the salt of the earth (Matthew 5:13). You are the salt, so be salty. You are the light, so let it shine! You are who you are becoming because of God's grace and mercy.

Max Lucado wrote, *"Our God is abundant in love and steadfast in mercy. He saves us, not because we trust in a symbol, but because we trust in a Savior."* [16]

Following His transfiguration, Jesus was met by a man with a son who was possessed by a spirit that had robbed him of speech. When the man told Jesus that his disciples could not drive the spirit out of his son, he told Jesus, *"if you can do anything, take pity on us and help us"* (Mark 9:22 NIV). Jesus immediately picks up the subtlety and asks, *"**If** you can? Everything is possible for one who believes"* (v. 23 emphasis mine). The boy's father then replies, *"I do believe. Help me overcome my unbelief"* (Mark 9:24 NIV)!

Even in our belief that Jesus is Lord and capable of anything, we can find ourselves at times in periods of disbelief, or unbelief. Too often the circumstances we find ourselves in will dictate to us our skepticism, when we are called by God to believe that He can even command the waves to be still (Mark 4:39). We should be dictating to our storms that Jesus is in control, rather than our storms dictating chaos to us.

So, label me a Christ follower; an imperfect sinner saved by God's amazing, limitless grace and seeking to be like my Master, Jesus Christ. If you fear labels have brought you to a place of being ineffective in life and in ministry, I pray *"the Lord of peace himself give you peace at all times and in every way"* (2 Thessalonians 3:16). If you fear labels all together, I pray the God of peace will sanctify you through and through (1 Thess. 5:23). For only in our sanctification can we be fully His, fully alive and truly understand God's grace as we cast out fear in our love for God (1 John 4:18).

We have been reconciled to God in order that we might be reconciled one to another.

Chapter 2

Revolution

"Try not to become a man of success. Rather become a man of value." – Albert Einstein

In 1968, The Beatles released their hit single, *"Revolution."* It was a time in our nation's history where many artists were taking the political and social issues up lyrically in their songs and painting their own artwork in music for the world to see. The opening verse of that song goes like this:

> *You say you want a revolution,*
> *Well, you know*
> *We all want to change the world*
> *You tell me that it's evolution*
> *Well, you know*
> *We all want to change the world.* [1]

Changing the world by way of godly influence through the power of Holy Spirit is the core of the Great

Commission. And yet Jesus never expected for that commission be carried out as a revolt. We know revolution to mean some type of forceful overthrow, an uprising against a group or a government – not what Jesus intended.

As Christ followers, we must be willing to revolt against the sin nature within each of us; the nature that James wrote about is continuously trying to drag us away and entice us. (James 1:14) It is a revolution that we must proclaim, an overthrow of the government of our own flesh, that wishes to be its own god with no consideration for the damage it inflicts on others, and even our own souls.

We have got to make a change. We have got to create an environment in our life that seeks to reverse the trends of selfishness and sin and replace them with love and obedience. We need a revolution. The very word *revolution* includes the word **love** in reverse order. Perhaps you have been traveling in a direction for so long and with such gusto that you have forgotten your first love and need to revolt against the brokenness you have embraced for so long.

Someone once said, *"We spend the first 40 years of our*

lives for success and the next 40 years for significance."
Over the past several years this statement has become
my life model along with John 3:30, *"He must increase,
but I must decrease."* In terms of gaining accolades and
awards, possessions and power, I have literally "been
there, done that, got the t-shirt."

Allow me to illustrate my point. While my wife and I
were careful not to have too large a debt load in our
early marriage, it was I that was in constant search for
more and more material things to line the walls of our
home in hopes of feeling some sense of satisfaction and
worth. I was also very quick to answer the phone when
the stream of calls came from other churches – bigger,
more "powerful" churches – to consider taking a
ministerial position. After all, it was the way of the
young pastor to excite the masses in hopes of being
recognized and wanted by other congregations with
larger crowds and bigger pay checks. At least that is how
I viewed it without giving conscious thought to it.

In the midst of my drive for more, my wife and I raised
two daughters. There was a strong sense of also
providing more and more earthly possessions for them in
order to not be seen as a slacking father, spending his

income on frivolous non-essentials; but bearing witness to the multitudes that I was a good provider for my family. But somewhere near my 40's I felt the shift; I realized a change was needed. A revolution was rising up in my own heart against the selfishness I had embraced.

While I am sure there are people who never learn the lessons I am about to reveal, I certainly did find myself realizing that there must be more to life than working to make money, only to spend that money on earthly possessions and ultimately have little or nothing to show for it; "stuff of earth," to quote the late Rich Mullins, that would eventually be left behind upon my death for someone else to sift through, selling to the highest yard sale bidder, or being offered on Ebay for fractions of what I had invested. I have seen plenty of people in my years of ministry who seem to never learn the life lessons that seem to come so easily for most everyone else.

I served with a pastor years ago who said, "Life is cheap tuition." At least it can be if those enrolled in the school of life are willing to pay attention to the intended lessons, learn from them and then apply them. The tests are sometimes very difficult, and we must have studied long and hard in order to pass them. It is the application stage that I think so many people have difficulty with. They simply are not willing to let go of tried and tested ways and embrace a new philosophy or learn from the mistakes of others. It is my hope that you are willing to listen, learn and apply what I am sharing to your life. As pastors we must be careful that we do not hear a truth just to pass it on to someone else, but that we make application first to our own lives, allow each truth to settle in our own soul, and take root in our own heart.

The shift in philosophy for me came as my daughters completed high school and began living on their own. My wife and I were empty nesters and had a lot of stuff to look at that we had accumulated over the years, but our lives seemed a bit empty, at least to me. I was coming to realize that there must be something more. And so, God began a work in my heart that would radically transform my outlook and focus. I moved from wanting another car every few months and answering the phone to every church that called to endeavoring to simplify my life.

In short, I want more life in my years than years in my

life. I want more quantity of love and significance than mere number of years. Do not get me wrong, I hope to live many years in order to lengthen my godly influence on others, especially my family. But if I die tomorrow, I hope that it can be said that I lived my life to honor God and to influence others to the same.

In my mid 40's, my wife and I attended a Dave Ramsey financial peace seminar at a local church. We both immediately realized the value in decreasing our albeit minimal debt and set a goal to be debt free, including our mortgage, by the time we turned 60 years old. Because of our diligence and God's faithfulness, we paid off our home at age 55, five years ahead of our goal! By then our daughters had married and were having children of their own and our focus moved from chasing success to being significant. We realized that we had to pour into the lives of our grandchildren and our children in order to be an effective witness to this new generation.

And so, the shift occurred; the primary focus of our lives now is not *stuff of earth*, but rather *significance of eternity*. How I wish younger couples could learn this lesson at an earlier age than we did; how I wish we had learned it sooner. But at least we have learned the lesson, and applied it, and now God is using us to demonstrate this truth to others.

We paraphrase Romans 13:8 like this, *"Owe no man but to love him."* It has become our mission statement as a couple, our mantra; and while we fall short often, it remains the central focus of who we believe we are called to be as Christ followers.

Let me be clear: I hate debt! (And I don't think God is very fond of it either.) Debt is a cancer to families, businesses and even churches and will eat away at your joy and even your faith. A major paradigm shift from success to significance occurred for me. And it can happen for you. How about it, fellow sojourner, do you want more life in your years than years in your life?

I have had a long love affair with cars and enjoy driving cars with manual transmission. Somehow it just seems like more power and control as I am able to determine when I shift from one gear to the next. When I think of a paradigm shift, I do not think of moving completely away from one philosophy to another, but rather using the momentum from one to move to the next. Like moving from second to third gear in a car, I have found that using the momentum of a life focused on success can be transitional to a life focused on significance.

In other words, I have not completely discounted success, but rather, now embrace a more heightened reality of living my life with meaning and purpose, now more than ever before. I still desire that my business is successful, for instance, so that I can continue to hire people and have godly influence in my community.

Success is necessary, but success is secondary. Success is not my primary objective – significance now is my chief focus, building off of the success that I have gained and the lessons I have learned.

You certainly have the power to determine what you give your life to; and you certainly have the power to determine when and even if you will make the shift from success to significance. But I can tell you from experience, life has more meaning now than ever before.

When my life was absorbed with success, I felt like my life was a treadmill that I could not stop or control. Life was moving at a blistering pace. It was as if someone kept bumping up the speed and the incline adjustments where I had no control at all. Life was like a runaway train. And I considered myself the engineer, but I could not control it anymore.

My greatest success is to realize the weight of my significance.

It took getting to the bottom of myself before I could learn that lesson. No one wants to hit rock bottom, but that is the way the Lord can most often get our attention. What you do when you bottom out is vital to your future and your integrity.

A moral failure occurred that cost me my ministry, reputation, salary and trust. I was bankrupt in every area of my life. Depressed and broke, I had no one to blame but myself. It was my fault, no one else's. I had not taken the time necessary to evaluate my life at critical passes, and now life was kicking me off the train for an extended period in the station. I had to start over. The climb out of the valley was long and arduous, but we made it. We put it all back together with God's help and in His time. And I can tell you that life has more meaning now than before, and, by God's grace, my wife and I have an even better marriage than before.

The **revol**ution I am speaking of is not an external rebellion or uprising, but a revolving from love of self to a place of our first love being God Himself. If you have been there and fallen, you can get back. While I thought God was my first love and told others He was, my actions proved differently. The spiritual revolution is the recapturing of love; it is to re-love; to love God first, to love others second and to love one's self through the lens of God's grace rather than the lens of man's judgmental labels.

Never have I known a Christ follower who wants to remain in the pit! To desire the pit is to desire emptiness and separation from God. You have got to climb your way out! It is your responsibility and no one else's!

If you will invest now and are willing to take some advice from a broken servant of God, you may find that you can avoid some of the pitfalls I succumb to, or, come back to an elevation of a greater understanding of His grace, mercy and power.

You Cannot Fly Solo

Let me add something here for clarification: significance is not a solo venture. You cannot create significance on your own. You are not Han Solo, and God does not honor that type of isolated, heroic, Lone Ranger behavior. If you are a pastor, you count on a team of staff and volunteers. If you are married you rely on your spouse. If you are in business you rely on your team of employees and perhaps a business partner. Nothing of significance has ever been accomplished solely by one person.

Consider any company or organization that is successful and though there may be one man or woman in the spotlight that receives most of the credit for the success, they are surrounded by a team that made the success possible. Even Christ's death on the cross calls for us to enter into partnership with God Himself to see the fruit of souls coming to know Him. So, when you consider your life of significance, please consider the help and input of those around you. You cannot fly solo! Please also consider the meaning your life can have on someone else who is walking in the light of God.

"Iron sharpens iron, and one man sharpens another" (Proverbs 27:17).

When we read Ecclesiastes 4:12, *"Though one may be overpowered, two can defend themselves. A cord of three strands is not quickly broken,"* (NIV) we tend to move directly to the third strand, the strand of God's presence.

But let us not neglect the consideration of the second strand, the strand of another person or perhaps a team that helps us all become whom God desires us to become.

Relying on others is not a sign of weakness, rather a statement of value – valuing others enough to involve them in your life and valuing yourself enough to share the load to avoid burnout; and, valuing the accountability that comes from involving others in your life.

You say you want a revolution? Well, we all want to change the world; let it begin with you.

Chapter 3

InTOXICating

"Never try to destroy someone else's life with a lie,
when yours can be destroyed with the truth." –
Anonymous

As a young newly enlisted private in the US Army, I was excited about the opportunities that Basic Training brought. One experience in particular really got the adrenaline going. As a part of our training, members of my platoon donned gas masks and were escorted into a gas chamber where CS gas, more commonly known as tear gas, was released. After standing in the chamber for a few seconds, we were to then remove our masks and exit the room in an orderly fashion, all the while coughing and gagging from the effects of the fumes. The exhilaration soon turned horrifying for me when I realized that as soon as I entered the gas-filled room, my

73

mask had not seated properly and was allowing the noxious fumes to immediately flow into my eyes and nose causing uncontrollable choking. The training event that I was so excited about quickly turned into a toxic nightmare.

The word *toxic* surely brings to mind dangerous symbols flashing before our eyes. Hearing the word *toxic* may invite images of the skull and cross bones symbol on many hazardous material containers. Perhaps you think of a nuclear power plant or other factories and plants that produce goods and have been found to pollute nearby streams and waterways.

While school children today sadly have active shooter drills, I was a child of the era of potential nuclear bombs being dropped by our adversaries. In our day, we had drills pertaining to hazards that were marked with special signs and plaques. We rightly think of poisonous, unsafe and even unfriendly environments wrought with peril and hazard when we think of the word *toxic*.

But when we wrap the word toxic inside the word *intoxicating*, somehow it loses its peril and becomes more exhilarating and exciting; more stirring and stimulating than dangerous and venomous. My intoxication for the Army training I was to receive, turned toxic in a matter of seconds.

This is exactly what can happen in relationships that we think are intoxicating – they can turn toxic in a hurry, or even be toxic from the start if we are not willing to safeguard our mind and heart, and set boundaries that will help define what a healthy relationship should look like.

Frankly, some unhealthy relationships can be both intoxicating and toxic. You may find the intoxicating thrill of the secret life with another person, when in fact, it is an extremely toxic, dangerous path that you walk, leading to and ending in great pain and turmoil.

I have known many alcoholics who would spend a great deal of time drinking with friends, and often times alone. Alcoholics feel a great sense of release of problems when they are drinking, but the downside is inevitable. Damaging effects to the body, hangovers and lost wages are among the pitfalls for those not willing to control their dangerous conduct, not to mention ruining one's family and perhaps doing time behind bars.

A friend of mine recently went through a very bad time

when he was arrested for a DUI and had outstanding warrants in three states. His license was revoked, and he spent months in the county jail. It was a horrible experience that actually taught him great life lessons as he reached the bottom of the pit physically, spiritually, emotionally and financially. He had a lot of time to contemplate his actions but with God's help and the help of the church, he is now on a better, new path of life. Sadly, he is among the minority of people who face what he has faced and come out on top. Many will never learn the lessons and will continue in destructive patterns until it is too late.

Alcohol is intoxicating; it can temporarily lift us out of and away from our trouble. But it is also toxic; it will destroy you and take down innocent people around you.

I knew a man in a church I pastored years ago who said that when he was a child he asked his father, "Dad, why don't we drink?" His father's words were so wise, "Son, I've seen alcohol ruin many a man, but I've never seen it make one." Whether you are a teetotaler or an occasional social drinker, you must realize that alcohol in excess is damaging and can even be deadly. But alcohol is not the only thing that can potentially rob us of our service and obedience to God.

There are certainly many intoxicating choices in this life, but the center of many of those things is toxic and deadly. I believe it was Ravi Zacharias who said, *"Sin will take you farther than you want to go, keep you longer than you want to stay, and cost you more than you want to pay."* How true. When caught in sin we realize what a high price we pay and what a great distance we travel, not to mention the price that those around us will pay.

National news has been filled in recent years with stories of toxic waste spills and companies have paid enormous fines for the carelessness with which they allowed those toxins to escape the boundaries of their organization into the environment. Toxic waste seeping into the ground and flowing into streams can have damaging and long-lasting effects on the environment and can reach far beyond the border of the offending agency that is guilty of the offense.

Too often we are guilty of dumping toxic waste into our own spiritual system. Spiritual toxic waste can come in a myriad of ways, but most often we simply become lazy or distracted and fail to manage the borders of our own spiritual life, allowing toxic ingredients to seep into our lives. And those toxic ingredients will flow out in various ways, sometimes continuing far beyond just the effect they have on us, but will flow to our loved ones and others, carrying with them damaging, sometimes irreversible effects.

Consider the television shows you watch, or the podcast that you listen to, or the internet sites that you visit, or the unhealthy conversations you engage in with others. Little by little you may have allowed toxic agents into your spiritual environment that may be doing damage that you are not even aware of; or you are aware of and just don't care.

When a person consumes so much alcohol that they become intoxicated, it impairs their judgement and their sense of reasoning; alcohol can literally change the behavior from rational it irrational.

The same is true for a Christian who eases too close to toxic relationships. We can exchange the truth of God for a lie and worship created things (Romans 1:25).

For many, the thing they find most intoxicating is self.

If you are reading this, you are probably being tempted

to stop at this point and put it down. *Enough is enough. I don't have a problem.* Right? Often times that is the case with us, we know ourselves so well, that we know we do not have the problems that we see lurking at the doorstep of so many others. But let me encourage you to resist the temptation to quit and keep moving forward. Too often people throw in the towel just before the victory is about to be won. So, my friend, don't stop! Keep going! There is something here for you that will bring radical change to your life and to your ministry.

The Lies We Buy

When my oldest daughter was nearing her sixteenth birthday, she had a particular car in mind that she wanted. My wife and I had promised to provide her with her first car and were anxious to get started looking at used vehicles with safety being our first priority. Unfortunately, the car our daughter wanted did not receive favorable reviews for safety and therefore, we could not buy her the car of her dreams.

In a society that will buy anything based on looks and the seductive labels, it becomes increasingly more difficult to convince the would-be buyer the difference between the marketing of a product, the reality of its safety and even the rationale of the purchase.

Romans says, *"They exchanged the truth of God for a lie"* (Romans 1:25 BSB).

It is easy for us to buy the deceits of our society and purchase products and services that may well over promise and under-deliver. My wife and I could have easily given in to the notion that car accidents are so sparse that nothing will ever happen to our daughter. But we listened to the warnings and went another direction. Accidents did follow for our young driver and I shudder to think of how things could have turned out if we had caved to the pressure and bought her the car she wanted. If you are not willing to be flexible and change directions, you are susceptible to exchanging the truth of God for the lies of the enemy.

The Author of Lies

I once knew a young man in a youth ministry I led years ago who had a severe lying problem; he was practically allergic to the truth. His problem was so great that he would lie when the truth would have been better. Lying, even though a sin, has become so acceptable a sin that it seems nearly everyone tells lies often. I have seen the increase in lying in younger generations, and they think little or nothing about lying to anyone at any time about anything.

No matter what kind of liar you have come across, there is no greater liar then the devil himself. Even the most habitual liar doesn't hold a candle to the lies the devil has perpetrated for centuries. After thousands of years of experience, fallen humanity continues to fall for the lies of the devil, even though they are as basic and fundamental as anything we know.

In John 10, Jesus gives us the three-pronged resume' of the enemy himself. He says, *"The thief comes only to steal and kill and destroy; I have come that they may have life, and have it to the full" (John 10:10 NIV).*

In the context of John 10, Jesus has referred to Himself as *"the gate."* The thief, Jesus says, *"is a robber,"* and *"climbs in* [the sheep pen] *some other way,"* other than the gate.

So, the thief will always try to convince us that there is a shortcut, another way around the Gate, instead of entering through the Gate, that is Jesus Himself. That is the role of God's enemy, the devil, to entice us to take detours around God's will and Word.

Consider the effort and scheming it takes to try to get into Jesus' sheep pen by trying to break in by some other means. Jesus is the Gate. Jesus is the Shepherd. Jesus is the Watchman. In short, Jesus is our all, for those who hear His voice and follow.

It is the thief who enters by other means than the gate, and it is the thief that attempts to convince others that entrance in any other way than the gate is acceptable. Our enemy is about the business of trying to convince us to go against the truth of Jesus' claim and persuade us to take the same bypass. And the devil's lies can sometimes be so subtle.

Jesus not only is the Truth, He will always tell you the truth, but the thief and robber will dishonestly try to enter another way, with mischief and deception. Those who enter by the Gate (Jesus) *"will be saved."* (John 10:9 NIV). Those who enter by any other means will be subjects of the devil who will *"steal, kill and destroy."*

There is no greater truth teller than God Himself, and there is no greater liar than the devil. Even Christ followers have to have careful discernment to recognize the subtleties of the scheme of the devil.

Shortly after I abruptly left the ministry because of my moral failure, God placed me in the presence of two wealthy and godly men. Both had walked similar paths than me and both several years my senior. We spent a lot of time together and honestly, it was my futile hope that I would learn something about them and their behavior that would help me increase my financial wealth, but God had something else in mind; He was going to use those two men to pour into me a spiritual wealth.

As we traveled in a truck for hours one day to a land development they owned, we talked about lying and I said, "It has been my experience that anyone who will lie for you will lie to you." Without missing a beat, one of the men said, "And anyone who will lie to you will lie about you." That is the truth.

After finishing high school, I spent a couple of years in the Army until I sensed God's call on my life to preach. I was a very young Christian, very green in the ways of the disciple, having not been discipled as I should have. One day I was not in the mood to go to work, not sick, just not in the mood, and I asked my wife to call the Army base and tell my supervisor that I was sick and would not be in that day. To her credit, my wife refused to make the call and lie for me. As upset as I was at her at that moment, now, I am so glad she did not lie for me, because it would have tarnished our relationship and trust. Had she lied for me in that moment, I would have questioned her truthfulness since. This is the truth:

Anyone who will lie for you, will lie to you; and anyone who will lie to you will lie about you. Never forget it.

Process the Process

I would like to encourage you to stop reading at this point and spend some sincere, honest time with God in prayer and the prayer of the Psalmist, *"Search me O God, and know my heart! Try me and know my thoughts! And see if there by any grievous way in me, and lead me in the way everlasting"* (Psalm 139:23-24)!

The wisdom of Proverbs is worthy to note here: *"Two things I ask of you; deny them not to me before I die: Remove far from me falsehood and lying; give me neither poverty nor riches; feed me with the food that is needful for me, lest I be full and deny you and say, 'Who is the LORD? or lest I be poor and steal and profane the name of my God'"* (Proverbs 30:7-9).

Do not hesitate to spend an extended time in honest, fervent prayer. God knows your thoughts, but He also knows your heart. I am sure your desire is to seek truth, so seek Him as Truth. God is not hiding from you; He can be found.

Remember the wisdom of Jeremiah, *"You will seek me and find me, when you seek me with all your heart."* (Jeremiah 29:13).

Chapter 4

It's a Trap

"You take me out of the net they have hidden for me, for you are my refuge." – Psalm 31:4

Years ago, my wife and I had a mouse that had found his home in our garage, feasting of dog food that we had carelessly let fall on the floor. Having found the fecal evidence that we had a rodent squatter sharing our space, I placed a cheese-bated trap in an area that I thought would catch him. It worked. I nailed the sucker!

What drew the unsuspecting vermin to the snare was his obvious thirst to feast and his familiarity with the delicacies I left. I had outwitted the mouse and removed him from his territory.

God's enemy has set a sumptuous yet basic trap in order to try to ensnare those of us who should know better, placing what he knows we desire in the trap as bate. He is constantly on the prowl to tempt us with things that he makes seem more attractive than they really are, and less harmful than they really are. Sin really will take you farther than you want to go, keeping you longer than you want to stay and cost you more than you are prepared to pay. That's the trap – that we do not believe any of that will be the case for us.

If you have ever had a mouse in your house you have tried to trap, you know that in order to ensnare the unsuspecting rodent, you have to bait the trap with something that will get its attention and draw it to the trap. The devil sets traps the same way, he uses something that will get our attention and that will draw us to the trap. But it is just that, a trap.

The truth is, Jesus not only *tells* the truth, He *is* the Truth (John 14:6), and there is no other means by which we may have true fellowship or union with Father except through Jesus, His Son. That verse is not just a "get to heaven" verse, it is a "have heaven with us while we are on earth" verse. You cannot have a secret lifestyle of sin and expect to walk with Jesus or expect Him to walk with you. Far too many people, pastors included, have tried to tight-rope their spiritual journey, teetering on the verge of falling, yet doing their best in their own power to hold it together. It is a duplicitous life. It is a trap!

There is an old southern gospel song by the Mark Trammel Quartet that has a timely and powerful chorus:

You know, your walk talks, and your talk talks
But your walk talks louder than your talk talks
Your behavior toward your neighbor
Is really how you feel about your Savior
When you exemplify and shine the Light of Christ
You know the number in the kingdom will be multiplied
You, your walk talks, and your talk talks,
But your walk talks louder than your talk talks.

Regardless of whether you are a pastor or not, if you are a Christ follower, your entire life is a sermon, being read one line at a time with every glance from other people. If you claim to be a follower of Jesus Christ, your entire life becomes evidence of your level of devotion to a watching world. Every word, every behavior, every decision, labels you and gives others a glimpse at our God, and it is up to you to make sure what people see is God our Father, and not the god of this age (2 Corinthians 4:4).

Though the devil is crafty and decent at setting traps, it is time we stop playing the game of "the devil made me do it," and realize that our choices are clear, enter through the gate and have life; or, by deception, try to enter by another means and suffer the consequences. Human beings have become masters at finding and creating detours, but there are no shortcuts to God's holiness.

The Message paraphrases Matthew like this, *"Don't look for shortcuts to God. The market is flooded with surefire, easygoing formulas for a successful life that can be practiced in your spare time. Don't fall for that stuff, even though crowds of people do. The way to life--to God!--is vigorous and requires total attention"* (Matthew 7:13-14 TM)

I worked for a while in our county jail and found that pre-trial inmates, those who are being held for some wrongdoing awaiting a court appearance, are always thinking about how to sneak out of the jail or sneak contraband in that they are not supposed to have. The heart of a person who tries to usurp the gate is a person of mischief, and cunning, and perhaps without even realizing it, is setting judgement against themselves.

Thieves lurk around in the cover of darkness trying to take something that does not lawfully belong to them; trying to find ways around the rules; trying to find ways to beat the system to satisfy their selfish, sinful desires. But people of integrity will always enter lawfully through the proper entrance, unless they accept the lies of the thief and try to gain entrance without going in the proper way. The greatest liar of all time, the father of lies, the devil himself, will try to convince us all that there are shortcuts around God's glory, around God's best, and the cost will be negligible. Adam and Eve learned the lesson by not heeding God's advice and they allowed the serpent to trick them and took the forbidden fruit from the tree in the center of the garden. (Genesis 2:9, 17).

Let us consider the trap the serpent set for Adam and Eve. It was for the eyes of these first two humans that he created the trap. Remember, Genesis says that *"the serpent was more crafty than any other beast of the field that the LORD God had made"* (Genesis 3:1). The devil used his own craftiness to set a trap for Adam and Eve.

There were at least five steps that led Adam and Eve to fall for the enemy's snare.

1. They looked at the forbidden fruit.

Looking may seem harmless, but it has been my

experience that when we look again and again, the devil uses those repetitive glances to continue to tempt us. We are left only to assume because the Bible does not clarify, but I have a feeling Adam and Eve did not take the fruit from the tree upon first glance; I can imagine that they circled the tree several times contemplating the powerful Word of the Lord versus the persistent temptation of the serpent. But even if they did take the fruit at first glance, it all started because they fell into the devil's trap of looking at what was forbidden. The Bible says that *"the woman saw that the fruit was good for food and pleasing to the eye."[1]* It was Eve's eyes that first caused her astray. The same holds true for David when *"he saw a woman bathing"* and sent someone to inquire about Bathsheba.[2]

Job knew the temptation of the gaze well and made a covenant with his eyes that he would not *"look lustfully at a young woman."* (Job 31:1 NIV). Face it, friend, God has created everything beautiful for our eyes to enjoy but when our heart runs ahead to take what does not belong to us, we have gazed too long. Which leads to the second point:

2. They realized it was beautiful.

As I said, I believe that everything God creates is beautiful. He has created everything for us to enjoy and for His own glory. He created man in His image; He creates everything else out of an abundance of His greatness. The line is crossed, however, when we look upon something so long that we begin to covet it, whether it be material possessions or fleshly desires. I can see a beautiful woman and recognize that she is beautiful, but the beauty God creates can be what the enemy uses to temp us.

When I was a newly born again teenager, an adult youth worker jokingly defined lust as looking at a woman twice, so he explained that he combatted that by seeing a beautiful woman and not taking his eyes off of her. Either way, a heart for God can be led astray, whether through a double take, or a fixed gaze. That man eventually divorced his wife for another woman because he could not control his eyes and he recognized something he thought more beautiful than the wife God had given him.

3. They desired the fruit.

And here comes the desire. I believe God created desire to reign in the hearts of men and women. Rightly placed, desire can be a wonderful thing when we desire the things that God would have us desire. Adam and Eve desired, they did not just recognize that the boundaries God had put in place were His will and for their protection; they desired to have the fruit after listening to the persuasive temptation of the enemy, even though God explicitly said it was off limits. If only Adam and Eve could have known and heeded Paul's caution, *"walk by the Spirit, and you will not gratify the desires of the flesh."* (Galatians 5:16). Desire always precedes action.

4. They acted upon their desire.

In the case of Adam and Eve, the Bible tells us that Eve tried the fruit and then gave some to her husband and he ate it too (Genesis 3:6). Often when we are caught in sin we have an accomplice, someone who has walked the path of wickedness with us. Of course, there are solo sins – those sins we commit without anyone else knowing, but in the case of so many sins, we commit with someone else. Which leads us to the next step:

5. They kept it a secret.

Adam and Eve realized they had sinned against God and sewed fig leaves to cover their nakedness. Until they sinned, they had not realized they were naked. Then, when they heard the sound of God coming through the garden, they hid among the other trees of the garden (Genesis 3:8). Admittedly, there was no one else to tell; they were the only two human beings on the planet. But in their sin, they thought they could hide from God, the very one who had given them life and everything they had.

Notice that Adam and Eve hid among the other trees in the garden, the very trees that God said they could enjoy. It's interesting to me that they were using the blessings of God to hide behind once they sinned. Consider the blessings that we hide behind when we sin.

You may hide behind the blessing of your reputation, or your position in the church that might be lost if someone knew the truth about your behavior. Both your reputation and your role in the church are because of the blessings of almighty God. And yet when we sin, like Adam and Eve, we hide behind the blessings of God when we have stolen from the tree that was off limits to us. We hide behind our blessings when we sin.

The two philosophies of the enemy and God could not stand in greater contrast: one comes to steal, to kill and to destroy. But One comes that we may have life; and not just life, but life to the fullest. One comes in secret; One comes in full disclosure. One comes in darkness; One comes as Light. One comes with lies, One comes *as* the Truth.

When it comes to sin, I am afraid the church has accepted the primus that all sins are the same, equal, if you will; that no sin is any greater than another; after all, we are all sinners in need of a Savior.

While it is certainly true that we are all sinners, and the only thing that gives us any hope is the death, burial and resurrection of Jesus Christ, it is not true that all sins are equal. Some sins carry far greater consequence than others; some sins do far more damage to body, soul and mind of the perpetrator, but also to those around them. I am afraid we have bought the lie that since all wrongdoing is sin, none are any greater than any other.

God destroyed cities for sexual sins, but I am not aware of a single city that God destroy because of the sins of gossip or gluttony.

The truth is God's sheep follow His lead because they know His voice. We can never know someone's voice if we do not hear it, and with God, we must hear it often. So, it becomes the task of the sheep to remain good listeners, seeking always to hear the voice of their Shepherd over all the other voices streaming our way from various directions with increasing velocity. Jesus' voice always speaks truth. Always. The enemy always ultimately speaks lies. While the enemy may have a nugget of truth, the overall intent is to lie – to steal, kill and destroy; to distort the truth for his own gain and your loss.

The devil used scripture (nuggets of truth, if you will) to tempt Jesus in the desert; he *misused* scripture in an attempt to trick Jesus.

Pastor, you are reading this, not to glean sermons or sermon ideas for your congregation. You must not read this with a discipleship or small group in mind. Though you might have a tidbit or two that you can work into a sermon or teaching setting at some point, the only reason for this publication is for your spiritual and moral benefit; that you may find tools to become stronger in your war against sexual sin – both the temptation and the act. The words found here are not for someone else, but for you.

Too often we spend time in study to tell other people how to live instead of studying to let God tell us how to live. We study to preach rather than study to apply.

In a way, this is an easy crowd to speak to; we are all pastors, and if we are not being truthful and honest, at least we know that we are supposed to be. We live from the perspective of the Bible, and though we have not lived sinless lives, and may not be living sinless lives now, we can all agree, at least, on absolute truth, where the world has lost that sense.

What gives me the right to speak to you? What are my credentials that allow me to speak to a group of pastors about failure? Hopefully in the course of the remainder of this book, you will learn the answer to that question and many more. Maybe you can find help before it is too late and change your course to avoid some of the painful pitfalls that I fell into. Paul wrote,

"Do you not know that the wicked will not inherit the kingdom of God? Do not be deceived: Neither the sexually immoral nor idolaters nor adulterers nor male prostitutes nor homosexual offenders nor thieves nor the greedy nor drunkards nor slanderers nor swindlers will inherit the kingdom of God" (1 Corinthians 6:9-10).

Ephesians 5:1-5, *"Be imitators of God, therefore, as dearly loved children and live a life of love, just as Christ loved us and gave himself up for us as a fragrant offering and sacrifice to God. But among you there must not be even a hint of sexual immorality, or of any kind of impurity, or of greed, because these are improper for God's holy people. Nor should there be any obscenity, foolish talk or coarse joking, which are out of place, but rather thanksgiving. For of this you can be sure: No immoral, impure or greedy person – such a man is an idolater – has any inheritance in the kingdom of Christ and of God"* (NIV).

Hebrews 13:4-8, *"Marriage should be honored by all, and the marriage bed kept pure, for God will judge the adulterer and all the sexually immoral. Keep your lives free from the love of money and be content with what you have, because God has said, 'Never will I leave you; never will I forsake you.' So we say with confidence, 'The Lord is my helper; I will not be afraid. What can man do to me?' Remember your leaders, who spoke the word of God to you. Consider the outcome of their way of life and imitate their faith. Jesus Christ is the same yesterday and today and forever."*

When it comes to marriage, I like Bill Perkins' illustration. As a small boy in Texas, Bill's father taught him how to ride horses. There were two important components to riding a horse: a saddle and a bridle. They each have different functions. Bill wrote, *"While the saddle helped me stay on a horse, the bridle enabled me to control an animal much larger and more powerful than me."* Marriage is like the bridle. Without it, our passions will run out of control, hurting us and others. [3]

In Galatians 5:19, Paul begins the list of *"acts of the sinful nature,"* with *"sexual immorality, impurity and debauchery."* God intended sex to be within the confines of the marriage covenant with one man and one woman. Mankind perverted that covenant.

The point is sexual sin carries with it far greater consequence and danger than any other sin. For those who think that all sin is equal, again, I challenge you to consider one city that God destroyed merely because of gossip. How about a city God destroyed solely because of lying? The truth is that sexual sin carries much greater penalties for the sinner as well as the society than any other sin.

Horses are, by nature, wild animals. In order to have the

ability to ride them and enjoy them, they have to be broken by a professional. Perhaps you have considered a broken person as unusable, someone that has had a chance to lead, but blew it and now is tossed aside.

But in reality to be broken as a man or woman in Christ means that we are submitting to our Master, just like a horse has been broken to obey the commands of its master. No one has gone too far to be rescued by our God. No one is beyond the reach of God's grace.

Let us be reminded of the words of Romans 8:38-39, *"And I am convinced that nothing can ever separate us from God's love. Neither death nor life, neither angels nor demons, neither our fears for today nor our worries about tomorrow—not even the powers of hell can separate us from God's love. No power in the sky above or in the earth below—indeed, nothing in all creation will ever be able to separate us from the love of God that is revealed in Christ Jesus our Lord."*

Allow me to encourage you to stop thinking of being broken as being used up, wasted, or unusable – separated from God. Consider what it means to truly be broken from the wild human nature, bent toward self and sin, and submit to the will of your Master.

Chapter 5

Character or Caricature

"The measure of a man is what he does with power." –

Plato

My wife and I enjoy visiting Gatlinburg, Tennessee at least once a year. That trip affords us the opportunity to get away and enjoy some uninterrupted time alone and to enjoy the beautiful creation of God in the mountains.

Like any city that seeks to draw tourists, there are caricature artists in the area in and around Gatlinburg. For a fee, they will draw a cartoon likeness of you complete with color accents and exaggerated physical features. Though we have never purchased a caricature of ourselves, we have been entertained by the artist's renderings of some of the people who have made purchases.

When it comes to character, I'm afraid we often have a caricature image of what godly character really should be, exaggerated. We have bought many lies from God's enemy regarding our behavior and what God tolerates and what He finds holy, acceptable and pleasing (Psalm 19:14). For many, character is not a noble pursuit, something we guide and frame by adherence to God's Word, but rather left to a chance happening for whatever becomes of us.

Character defines what we value morally, ethically and even spiritually with the Word of God as our source. The Bible offers some examples for the framework of godly character.

- Ruth was *"a woman of noble character"* (Ruth 3:11 NIV).

- Proverbs says that a wife of noble character is *"the crown to her husband"* (Proverbs 12:4 NRSV).

- Jesus' disciples noticed that Jesus was "a man of integrity," and taught "the way of God in accordance with truth" (Matthew 22:16 NIV).

How do you define character? Depending on the author, character can be viewed from very different perspectives. Some are said to lack character while others are described as men or women of great character. Some may say that we have no control over our character while others would say that we are in complete control of our character.

Abraham Lincoln said, *"Character is like a tree and reputation like a shadow. The shadow is what we think of it; the tree is the real thing."*

Clearly our lives must take root in something; whether a Christian or an atheist, we all have something that guides us and that will help in defining who we are and what we value. That could be the tree that Mr. Lincoln spoke of. And our reputation will likely be reflective of what we value. What we hold dear, we generally spend time with, spend time doing, or spend time pursuing.

The reputation is witnessed in public but is established in private. Who we are in private is the very essence of who we are in reality. Pride is developed in our alone time only to be shown in our actions when we are in community with others.

In 2005, country music star, Leann Womack, released a song entitled, *Stubborn*, on her album, There's More

Where That Came From.

See if you can identify with the lyrics:

There's a whole lot of stubborn in this room
There's a whole lot of pride that won't let go
There's a whole lot of stubborn in this room
That shows no sign of giving up control
I've drawn all the curtains
I've turned out all the lights
Scared to death somebody else might see
There's a whole lot of stubborn in this room
And there's no one here but me [1]

The Devil's Lies

It is your character that the devil is after. The enemy of God would love to destroy the reputation of every proclaiming Christ follower by influencing each of us to give way to our convictions and in so doing, make choices that would tarnish our reputations. He will feed us lies in order for us to compromise our biblical stance and drift to other standards. It has been my experience that the enemy lies to us in five major ways. These lies can be applied to any area of life, but especially in the arena of sexual temptation and sexual sin.

Before we study the five lies of the devil (Chapter 6), let us look at the temptation of Jesus as we lay the groundwork for the devil's schemes.

Matthew 4 tells the story.

Jesus was hungry after He was led into the desert by the Spirit to be tempted by the devil, and the devil tempted Him first at His greatest area of need – physical nourishment. I have found that the enemy can bring intense temptation at our weakest moments; at the moments when we are hungry, either for a bite to fill our stomach, or the Word of God to fill our soul. Following a 40 day fast, food can be a tremendous temptation.

Having experienced a few long-term fasts, I can tell you that temptation is fierce during those times, but there is also a greater sense of one's need to press into the Father.

Jesus' second temptation by the devil was to throw Himself off the highest point of the temple to be rescued by angels. I have found that the enemy can bring incredible temptation when we are at our greatest moments. When all is at its zenith, beware; the devil prowls around, seeking whom he may destroy. [2]

When a church is experiencing numeric growth, it can be a time of great testing and temptation for pastoral leadership. The humanity of any pastor can be in danger of taking credit for things best left for the glory of God. You may consider numeric growth in a church a sign that you are doing it right, and therefore be tempted to elevate yourself, even to a position above God.

By the way, that is why Peter admonished us to be *alert and watchful* in 1 Peter 5:8. That verse is also written in the context of Peter's appeal to elders and young men.

The third temptation of the devil to Jesus was to have full control of all the kingdoms of the world if only Jesus would bow down to worship him. I have found that the enemy can make big promises, but never makes big deliveries. He never delivers because he cannot deliver. He had no power to deliver the kingdoms of the world to Jesus; Jesus was already the Son of God and owned all the kingdoms of the world. The lie of the devil is for you to lose sight of what you have by making it feel like it is no longer enough.

Each of the temptations of Jesus teach us something about the character of the devil, but also the character of God.

Bill Perkins refers to our sinful appetites as our dragon within. He writes, "The dragon within wants one thing:

total domination of your life (Romans 7:23). And it will use God's law to enslave you." [3] The devil attempted to use God's Word against God's Son to tempt Him; and do not think he will not use the Word of God in the same way to tempt you.

The devil is a master at promising what he cannot deliver, and so often making promises against what you already have. God's enemy can make no promise that he can keep, he can only produce lies in order to remain valid to his resume, to steal, to kill and to destroy.

The Character of the Devil

Peter wrote, *"Your enemy the devil prowls around like a roaring lion looking for someone to devour."*[4] The character of the devil is stair-stepped with empty promises, each greater than the one before, as we see in the devil's temptations of Jesus. The devil will often times even misuse Scripture to convince us, just as he did with Jesus; those lies are exaggerated caricatures of what God's image of us is and what He expects.

The character of the devil is to pit God against man, and man against God. The devil is the enemy of God and the enemy to mankind.

The character of the devil is to tempt with a very present need to show his cunning; but his promises are empty. Notice that the devil did not claim to *give* Jesus bread, but tempted Jesus to do what He really could have done, but for the wrong motive and from the wrong voice and turn the stones into bread Himself.

Jesus could have turned rocks into bread, after all, He turned water into wine (John 2:1-11). The devil could **not** have turned the rocks into bread; that is why he tempted Jesus to do it. The devil can never keep a promise.

John says that when the devil *"lies, he speaks out of his own character, for he is a liar and the father of lies."* [5]

The character of the devil is to promise far more than he can deliver. The devil was tempting Jesus with something He already had, rule over all the kingdoms of the world, if only Jesus would bow down and worship the devil. We do not ever seem to be that thoughtful in our sin, that we are *bowing* down to the devil, but essentially, that is exactly what we are doing when we sin; we are surrendering our fatherhood of God as our Father and turning it over to the devil as our father.

The Jews of Jesus' day protested that as descendants of Abraham, they had never been slaves to anyone when Jesus insisted that holding to His teachings would be proof that they were His disciples. While they claimed that their only Father was God, Jesus insisted that they belonged to their father, the devil (John 8:31-4).

Three desert temptations by the devil with three empty promises, and three solid, Scriptural answers by Jesus with a final, *"Away from me!"* command. And because of Jesus' persistence, the Bible says, *"the devil left him, and angels came and attended him"* (Matthew 4:11 NIV).

Perhaps we would do well to learn that the Word is our sword, living and active (Hebrews 4:12), and we have the power to tell the devil to "go to hell!" where he belongs. The devil only has as much power over your life as you submit to, no more.

The devil is always about his business, we must always be about our Father's business.

The Character of God

God's character could not stand in more contrast than the character (if you can call it that) of the devil.

Where the devil makes promises he cannot keep, *"all God's promises are yes and amen in Christ."* [6] The problem for most pastors is that we are seeking for God to answer promises He never made. God never promised that your congregation would grow larger in number if you just preach better sermons. God never promised that the members of your church would stand and applaud your flawless homilies. God never promised that you would be widely respected by others. God never promised that your life would be easy if you would just submit to His call. God makes only promises He intends to keep; and keep them He does. That is His character.

God's character is defined in Who He is and by what He promises:

God is love (1 John 4:8)
God is just (2 Thessalonians 1:6)
God is holy (1 Peter 1:16)
God is an ever-present help in our time of need (Psalm 46:1)
God will never leave us nor forsake us (Hebrews 13:5)
God is merciful (Ephesians 2:4)
God is powerful (Psalm 71:18)
God is righteous (Psalm 11:7)
God is sovereign (Luke 1:37)
God rules (Psalm 103:19)
God reigns (Psalm 99:1)
God controls the seasons (Genesis 1:14)
God created all that is from nothing (Genesis 1:1)

God is faithful (1 Corinthians 1:9)

I think I know why the late Rich Mullins penned the words, *"Our God is an awesome God, He reigns from Heaven above with wisdom, power and love, our God is an awesome God."* [7] Just reading the Bible promises is enough for me. As the old hymn says, "He never has failed me yet."

We always have command over the devil when we speak scripture and when we remain steadfast in our resolve to *"Worship the Lord your God, and serve him only"* (Matthew 4:10 NIV). The devil has no authority over you. You surrender your authority to the devil when you give way to temptation.

You may have heard it said this way, "The only thing you need to do to remain in God's will is to do the next right thing." That is why it is critical to remain in close, intimate fellowship with Jesus in a continual state of prayer and communion with Father.

God cares deeply for you. His heart breaks with yours and He longs for you to have the deepest, most intimate relationship with Him possible. God does not desire that your joy be contingent on your circumstances, but on

His character. Our part is to remain faithful, committing to do the next right thing.

Many pastors are a mere pencil drawing, a caricature of the image they want to portray. Innuendos were a big part of my downfall; you know, those seemingly innocent comments we make in order to make people laugh. After all, if I can make you laugh, perhaps you will hear what I have to say; perhaps you will like me. I was a caricature, a cartoon drawing of what God wanted me to become.

"Bad company ruins good morals" (1 Corinthians 15:33). In other words, the company we keep can do damage to our character and our moral outlook. Equally, we can have an adverse effect on those that keep company with us if we do not learn to keep our humor and insinuations at bay.

Paul wrote to the church in Ephesus, *"Let there be no filthiness nor foolish talk nor crude joking, which are out of place, but instead, let there be thanksgiving"* (Ephesians 5:4).

I would encourage you to take a close inventory of your speech to see if there is any in you that is offensive to

God (Psalm 139:24). Your character demands it. Your influence on the character of others demands it. Our speech is born from our heart; our heart is framed by our mind. It is not just for children to be reminded, *"Be careful little eyes what you see, be careful little ears what you hear."* It is for those of us who have been called to shepherd God's people that we learn to keep a tight rein on our tongue and a guard posted at the doorway of our mind and our heart. After all, Jesus said, *"what comes out of the mouth proceeds from the heart, and this defiles a person"* (Matthew 15:18).

Chapter 6

The Tricks of the Traitor

"Educating the mind without educating the heart is no education at all." - Aristotle

So, with that in mind, let us look at how the devil will tempt us and try to convince us that our sin is justified. Even those little "meaningless" jokes and inferences that can have devastating effects come from the devil himself.

Proverbs 4:23-27 lists our *heart*, *tongue*, *eyes* and *feet* as the parts of the body that we must guard or keep wholly unto God.

The NIV renders these verses like this:

²³ Above all else, guard your heart,

for everything you do flows from it.

²⁴ Keep your mouth free of perversity;

keep corrupt talk far from your lips.

²⁵ Let your eyes look straight ahead;

fix your gaze directly before you.

²⁶ Give careful thought to the paths for your feet

and be steadfast in all your ways.

²⁷ Do not turn to the right or the left;

keep your foot from evil.

Let's look at four phrases from this Proverb:

1. Guard your heart (v. 23)
2. Keep your mouth free of perversity (v. 24)
3. Let your eyes look straight ahead (v. 25)
4. Give careful thought to the paths for your feet (v. 26)

Interestingly, each of those Proverb verses has a New Testament complement, a modern-day interpretation for what the Old Testament wisdom revealed.

1. We guard our hearts by loving God with our whole heart and others as ourselves (Matthew 22:37-39).
2. We keep our mouths free from perversity by guarding our tongues (James 3:1-12).
3. We let our eyes look straight ahead by fixing them on Jesus (Hebrews 12:2).
4. And we give careful thought to the paths of our feet by walking in a manner worthy of the calling we have

received (Ephesians 4:1).

Our whole being must be under the complete and utter control of Holy Spirit. Nothing can be left for us to manage on our own, because we have a way of perverting anything we are left alone to. Without God's presence in every area of our life, we will fail at some point, on some level. It is vital that we have confidence and courage in our call in order that we may "extinguish all the flaming arrows of the evil one" (Ephesians 6:16 NIV).

With that, here is my list of the five greatest lies the devil tells.

1. It isn't really a sin until you commit the physical act.

Let us face it, we all have a difficult time drawing the line between when temptation becomes sin. Often times sinful thoughts are dismissed, and things like viewing pornography are set aside, when in reality the very act of viewing pornography, though we haven't *physically* committed a sin with our body, we have committed a sin with our eyes in viewing pornographic material. (our eyes are part of our body.) The enemy, in his craftiness, will try to convince us that some sins really are not sins, or, that some sins are acceptable because they are not

119

seemingly as bad as other sins.

2. If lust of the heart is a sin, you may as well go ahead and commit the physical act.

The devil will attempt to convince you that your thoughts are your business, private and known to no one else. But since you are a Christian and you know that God's Word says that lust in the heart is adultery (Matthew 5:28), the devil will convince you that you have already sinned, so what's the difference. The thought may be something like this, "Well, since I've already sinned by lusting in my heart, I may as well go ahead and enjoy the pleasure of the sin with my body." Another one of the lies the devil has sold to countless Christ followers that will ultimately destroy intimacy with God and with others, especially one's spouse.

3. You will be able to separate your secret life from your public life without any impact on your ministry.

One of the most crafty lies of the devil is that we can compartmentalize our lives like rooms in a house. There may be some rooms in your house that you do not allow guests to enter – rooms filled with junk or that are just too dirty and unkempt. The lie of the devil is that you can keep those activities (rooms) separate from other activities (rooms) and no one will have to see them or even know about them. A lot of men and women have lived in duplicity thinking that their sin was theirs alone and no bother to anyone else.

Richard Dortch wrote, *"Almost every person that I can think of who has fallen – whether layman or minister – did so because they believed they were the exception. They thought they could pick and choose when and how to sin – even only if occasionally and for a good cause – and it would make no difference. Their public persona portrayed what they wanted everyone to believe was true about them. They convinced themselves that no one would see the other side of their life."* [8]

Sin disguises itself under the appearance as something that is good. How could it be sin for a man who has not eaten in 40 days to turn a stone into bread? That is the allure, if you are hungry, you must eat no matter the cost.

4. No one will find out.

Every lie the devil tells is framed with the lie that no one will know. Remember, Jesus was alone in the desert with the devil when He was tempted to turn stones into bread. How easy it is to sin when we are alone, thinking that no one will ever find out. Numbers 32:23 says, *"be sure that your sin will find you out."* [9] Even alone, great damage can be done to one's spirit by involvement in "alone sin."

5. No one will be hurt.

Who would have been hurt if Jesus had heeded the temptation of the devil and thrown himself down from the highest point of the temple? Aside from Jesus being the sinless promised Messiah sent to pay for the sins of all of humanity, perhaps no one would have been hurt – at least that is what the devil would have us believe. But the ripple effect of our sin is always far greater than the enemy tells us. Sexual sin will not only affect your own body, soul and mind, it will seep out to those around you with crushing consequences.

Sin, even private sin, will affect you. And it will have sometimes even greater effect on those around you. Consider the spouse and children of a cheating pastor. Their lives could be completely altered at no fault of their own; they could become homeless, fatherless and destitute all because of the actions of another person, not to mention the public shame from the actions of such a high profiled community leader.

When I was a child my family lived in the country on a couple of acres of land. We grew a garden on one acre and lived on the other. (If you don't think a one-acre garden is a big garden then I challenge you to try it sometime.) But let's say that we planted corn in the ground and expected tomatoes to grow from that ground. How foolish. The Bible is clear that we reap what we sow and nothing else. If you sow corn in the ground, you will *only* reap corn from that seed. If you sow sin in your life, do not expect to reap anything other than the penalty of God for that behavior. Although sin may go hidden for a season, be sure, your sins will always find you out (Numbers 32:23).

Galatians 6 says, *"Do not be deceived: God is not mocked. For whatever one sows, that will he also reap. For the one who sows to his own flesh will from the flesh reap corruption, but the one who sows to the Spirit will reap from the Spirit"* (Galatians 6:7-8).

Be assured, it will not stop with you. If you *choose* to commit egregious sexual sin, the affects will be great upon your family, your church and those close to you.

And I do mean *choose*; no one ever commits sexual sin by accident. Walking disobediently into sin will cost you greatly and will bring unimaginable pain to those you love the most.

Sexual sin never happens by accident. Sure, there may be a "chance encounter" that turns into a "one-night stand," but in reality, there are always numerous opportunities to take an off ramp and run. If we are not constantly vigilant, we will not only fall prey to the snares of the enemy, we will place ourselves in predicaments that will allow for overwhelming temptation.

God will always provide a way out for those who are attentive to His voice.

1 Corinthians 10:13, *"No temptation has overtaken you except what is common to mankind. And God is faithful; he will not let you be tempted beyond what you can bear. But when you are tempted, he will also provide a way out so that you can endure it"* (1 Corinthians 10:13 NIV).

Here is the reality of sin and how it leaves you lacking:

- If you believe that your sin has no effect on others,

then you lack <u>knowledge</u>.

- If you believe that your sin will not be known, then you lack <u>wisdom</u>.

- If you believe that your sin can be compartmentalized, then you lack <u>understanding</u>.

- If you believe that your sin is no one else's business, then you lack <u>accountability</u>.

Allow me to offer scriptures for a better understanding of what I have just written above.

- Proverbs 24:3-4, *"By wisdom a house is built, and through understanding it is established; through knowledge its rooms are filled with rare and beautiful treasures."*

- Proverbs 3:19-20, *"By wisdom the Lord laid the earth's foundations, by understanding he set the heavens in place; by his knowledge the deeps were divided."*

- Proverbs 2:6, *"For the LORD gives wisdom and from his mouth come knowledge and understanding."*

- James 5:16, *"Therefore, confess your sins to one another and pray for one another, that you may be healed. The prayer of a righteous person has great power as it is working."*

How Did I Get Here?

If you are involved in sexual sin, you may wonder how you allowed it to happen. Something happens to our mind and our heart when we sin. Jesus said that we must love God with our whole heart, soul, mind and strength (Matthew 22:37). Sexual sin always begins in the heart and mind. That is why it is so essential to guard your heart and mind at all costs, not giving up for a second to the temptations from the enemy of God.

Sexual sin always involves:

1. A Scheming Heart – when the Bible says, *"Do not covet your neighbor's wife"* (Exodus 20:17), it means do not "desire" or "take delight in something that is outside of the acceptable bounds of God." Coveting arises from two sources: a perception of beauty and a desire to possess it, and a persistence for power. So, the heart can be set in motion to scheme on how to achieve what the heart desires.

2. A Seared Conscience – in 1841 Charles Finney wrote that conscience is not the mere knowledge of right and wrong but is an act of the mind and a judge that convicts

the mind; and the conscience becomes seared by will resisting the affirmations of reason. Finney says that the evidences of a seared conscience are the apathy on moral subjects.

In the following chapters we will look at how it is possible to surrender our conscience to the culture as we in effect cease to be the church that God desires, the bride of Christ.

Chapter 7

Conscience and Culture

"To lead the orchestra, you have to turn your back on the crowd." – Max Lucado

God is not sitting as a judge to hear arguments from lawyerly types to consider where His Word is valid in an ever-changing culture. God's Word is black and white; not open for debate or polling to make changes as the society around us changes. Yet we are guilty of allowing some things that God ordains as holy to become unholy because of societal pressure and our own inability to stand up for what we know to be right. We are not unlike the audience that Paul wrote the book of Romans to: We have *"exchanged the truth about God for a lie, and worshiped and served created things rather than the Creator—who is forever praised."* (Romans 1:25 NIV).

We have accepted wrongdoings, what God calls sin, and

called them right.

We have accepted these forms of wrongdoing in three arenas:

- Our Conscience,
- Our Culture and
- The Church.

We have accepted the lie to think like the world. We accepted the lie to act like the world as we see the culture invading the church. We have accepted the lie to allow the Church to be influenced by the culture more than the Church influencing the culture. All three are sinful behavior. Let us look at each one more closely.

Conscience

I'll begin with conscience, dealing with it extensively, and touch on culture and church in later chapters.

Proverbs 23:7, *"As a man thinketh in his heart, so is he"* (KJV). Notice the passage says, "so **is** he," not, "so **as he does**."

The Hebrew verb there means, *"to estimate,"* or *"to calculate."* [1] In fact, the ESV renders that verse, "he is like one inwardly calculating." This verse is speaking of the person who is calculating in his thought process.

So often we allow our sin nature to define who we are, and in so doing, give way to our sin nature in the form of our actions. We guard our minds because our thoughts produce beliefs which are sometimes defined in our actions. We guard our minds to eventually control our actions. Essentially your thoughts, if they are calculating, can give way to your sin nature and therefore bring ungodly conduct. We are all sinners, born enemies of God in need of a Savior. The nature I am speaking of is the core of who you are based on what you allow into your mind and heart. Dieticians would say, "You are what you eat." Christ says, "You become what you give your mind and heart to."

Consider this: Some people can act in certain ways enough to fool others, but that will soon wear off.

If I were to assemble a bunch of pastors in one room and go around that room asking every one of them "who are you," all would likely reply, "I'm a pastor." You define yourself by what you do, the Bible defines you by what you think in your heart; and for some of us, it is calculating thinking rather than pure thinking.

Our thoughts are where our actions stem from. Our thoughts are where the devil attacks us, and the devil

131

attacks truth in our minds. That is where it started for Adam and Eve in the Garden, and that is where it starts for you and me. We do not know who we are.

In terms of our calling as pastors, we too often try to do before we know who we are. Who you are in Christ is imperative to what you do for Christ. Far too many pastors and Christians alike are attempting to serve Christ without knowing who they are in Christ. I do not do what I do as a pastor in order to become who I am supposed to be; but because of who I am, and more importantly, Who's I am. I do what I do through the power of Holy Spirit at work in my life. Holy Spirit is not a luxury, He is a necessity. Holy Spirit is not an addendum to my life, He is the contents and the conclusion. Everything I am and ever hope to be is completed in His work in my life. You and I can accomplish nothing of lasting value and worth without the presence of Holy Spirit in our lives.

We must learn as Zechariah did when the LORD said to him, *"'It's not by might, nor by power, but by my Spirit' says the LORD Almighty"* (Zechariah 4:6).

Galatians 5:22-23 embodies the fruit of the Spirit of God. Those are the evidences of the presence of the Sprit in our lives, not a mere checklist of things we are to accomplish within our own. I would challenge any pastor to spend some extended time in those two verses and ask God to reveal to you where you are lacking. It might just be that you simply do not know who you are in Christ.

The Word of God says we must be transformed by the renewing of our mind because it is the mind that is transformative.

Consider these powerful scriptures:

"You were taught, with regard to your former way of life, to put off your old self, which is being corrupted by its deceitful desires; to be made new in the attitude of your minds; and to put on the new self, created to be like God in true righteousness and holiness." (Ephesians 4:22-23 NIV).

"Therefore we do not lose heart. Though outwardly we are wasting away, yet inwardly we are being renewed day by day." (2 Corinthians 4:16 NIV).

Consider Adam and Eve again. Death, biblically speaking, is a separation from God. When Adam and Eve sinned by taking the fruit from the tree in the middle of the garden, they were pronouncing upon themselves the death that God had promised in Genesis 2:17. It was not a physical death for they continued to live for many, many years; what they experienced was a spiritual death. And because of the spiritual death they suffered the unseen things became the seen things. They had seen the trees in the garden, but they had not seen the evil that could be unleashed on humanity until they ate of the tree of knowledge.

God's intent was to protect Adam and Eve, but because of their sin their conscience was exposed to evil. Any time we sin, and our conscience is exposed to God, we tend to want to hide from God, just as Adam and Eve, but the damage of the death, separation, has already occurred.

When Adam and Eve were exposed, they tried to hide from God by sewing fig leaves together and covering themselves in order to hide from God. Any time we knowingly transgress God's law we desire to cover it up. As much as we are hiding from God when we die in our sinful behavior, we are also attempting to hide from ourselves, our own conscience.

If you think that you cannot be tempted in this area then

chances are you are full of pride and that is exactly where the enemy wants you in order to do the most damage to your ministry.

None of us were born preachers, we were all born sinners. We became preachers not because of anything special in and of ourselves, but because of the grace and call of God, and that only.

In Proverbs Solomon gave strong words for young men considering adultery. *"Now then, my sons, listen to me; do not turn aside from what I say. Keep to a path far from her, do not go near the door of her house, lest you give your best strength to others and your years to one who is cruel, lest strangers feast on your wealth and your toil enrich another man's house. At the end of your life you will groan, when your flesh and body are spent. You will say, "How I hated discipline! How my heart spurned correction! I would not obey my teachers or listen to my instructors. I have come to the brink of utter ruin in the midst of the whole assembly"* (Proverbs 5:7-14 NIV).

Twenty five percent of men who commit adultery ruin their families financially. Consider what happens to preachers who often times have nothing to fall back on monetarily and have to take low paying jobs when removed from their pulpit. I think that percentage is greater for preachers.

Titus declares, *"To the pure, all things are pure, but to the defiled and unbelieving, nothing is pure; but both their minds and their consciences are defiled"* (Titus 1:15).

Question: Can a Christian view pornographic material and remain pure in thought?

Obviously, the answer is no. Then why do so many Christians, even pastors, behave like "the defiled and unbelieving?"

We have been sold a bill of goods, and we have bought it hook, line and sinker. We think that we must think like the culture thinks rather than how the Bible teaches, in order to reach the culture. And so, it has been a slow drift from the Word of Truth to the ways of temptation. Admittedly the pornography illustration is an extreme position, but there are many other lesser ways that we have rolled over to the beliefs of society.

For some of us, we need to literally recalibrate our minds to the Word of God because we have drifted so far from the Truth of God that we hardly recognize it anymore. Sadly, so many that have drifted, don't even realize they have drifted. Being off by just a few degrees from God's Word can affect behavior and leave us dead spiritually speaking.

Consider a barista's thermometer. It must be accurately calibrated to 32 degrees in order to have a consistent temperature at 160 degrees to make that latte enjoyable. Recalibrating our minds to the sensitivity of Holy Spirit and the Word of God is much the same, lest we position ourselves to become vulnerable to the craftiness of the enemy.

Allow me to share with you five things that I am convinced of regarding the conscience.

1. Conscience is an internal spiritual gyroscope that integrates to one's value system.

A gyroscope is a mechanism that helps maintain an aircraft's attitude (the orientation of the aircraft to the horizon).

When an aircraft is operating it is constantly facing forces coming at it from various directions. Gravity and wind can affect the craft's yaw, pitch and roll. The plane is continually judging the external forces and making instantaneous changes in order to remain stable and fly properly without crashing. That is the effect of the gyroscope.

The information from the gyroscope is relayed to the motor control drivers which in turn control the speed of the motors. So, it compensates the change in position in such a way that the aircraft basically seems unaffected as it re-adjusts its position hundreds of times every second. This is how planes tolerate winds and hover smoothly.

In aircraft, altitude is position, attitude is orientation. Airplanes use instruments for altitude (distance from ground) and attitude (how the aircraft is directed toward the horizon) to direct the pilot to fly in such a way that is most safe and will avoid danger.

As Christ followers our attitude should be the same as that of Christ Jesus (Philippians 2:5), fixed on the horizon of the Father. Christ followers have a built in gyroscope that must be monitored regularly to assure that they have their eyes fixed on Jesus (Hebrews 12:2).

As a pastor, here are a few things to remember:

- To be an effective leader, you must first be a committed follower. David had a heart after God's own heart (Acts 13:22).

    o Do you have a heart after God's heart? Our culture has far too much pride in the pulpit; we need more of God's heart in the pulpit.

- To be an effective leader you must have a servant's heart. Moses' leadership was so effective because he was *"the servant of God"* (1 Chronicles 6:49).

    o Are you a servant of God? Or are you merely expecting the congregation to serve?

- To be an effective leader you must be an effective visionary. Proverbs says, *"where there is no vision, the people perish"* (Proverbs 29:18 KJV).

    o Are you a visionary? Many pastors are asking congregations to follow a parked car.

- To be an effective leader you must be an effective teacher. Paul warned Timothy, *"Pay*

close attention to yourself and to your teaching"
(1 Timothy 4:16 NASB).

- o Are you a biblical teacher? Many pastors are preaching cultural topics with shallow or no substance rather than the inerrant, infallible Word of God.

- To be an effective leader you must be equipping God's people for ministry (Ephesians 4:11-12).

- o Are you purposefully equipping your flock? Far too many pastors are content to have a congregation of unequipped sheep as long as the numbers are there. Discipleship is very difficult work, taking time and intentionality.

- To be an effective leader you must be prayerful. Paul wrote that we must, *"pray in the Spirit on all occasions with all kinds of prayers and requests. With this in mind, be alert and always keep on praying for all the Lord's people."* (Ephesians 6:18 NIV).

- o Have you evaluated your prayer life lately? How easy it is to drift in this area with all the busyness in our schedules. Don't let it happen.

So, how about it pastor?

- Are you a committed Christ follower?
- Do you have a servant's heart?
- Do you have a Spirit-led vision for the flock that God has entrusted you with?
- Are you teaching the Word of God and intentionally equipping God's people?
- Do you have a regular, consistent, sincere prayer life?

Honest (and truthful) answers to those questions could put you back on a path of being the godly leader of the flock that God intends you to be. Answering "no" to any of those questions could mean that you are in dire need of a spiritual renewal in your own life.

It is not my role to question your call or cause you to question your call; only to spur you on to love and good works (Hebrews 10:24). I pray that you will receive the gentle nudging of a brother who has had it all, lost it all, and now counts the cost more than ever before.

Michael Hyatt and Daniel Harkavy wrote in their book, *Living Forward*, "Self-leadership always precedes team leadership." [2] If you are not effectively leading yourself you will fail in your efforts to lead others. In short, if you are not leading yourself to your prayer room, you will never be effective in leading others there.

The enemy is deceiving; that is his purpose and strength. Do not allow him to take your eyes off of the instrument panel of God's love and grace.

- Pay attention to God's Wisdom.
- Pay attention to God's Word.
- Pay attention to God's Will.

God really is an ever present help in our time of need. (Psalm 46:1). His voice is still and small, you must listen with purpose and intent. God whispers through our prayers to His people. Can you hear Him?

Give God the right to give you His revelation.

Chapter 8

Avoiding the Crash

"The Jews looked upon a serpent to be freed from serpents; and we look upon the death of Christ to be delivered from death." – Augustine

Though I am not a pilot, I have studied aircraft instrument panels for some time. I am fascinated with how we can apply what we know about aircraft cockpit instrumentation to how we must live as Christ followers.

Let us take a look at each gauge in on the instrument panel and make application to our spiritual journey as pastors.

1. Altimeter – also called the altitude indicator *judges the distance between the aircraft and the ground, calculated with current barometric pressure.*

APPLICATION: pressure will rise and fall in the ministry causing us to rise and fall with the environment. But a good altimeter will keep you at the right altitude.

One of my favorite Old Testament scriptures is Isaiah 40.

²⁹ He gives power to the weak,
And to those who have no might He increases strength.
³⁰ Even the youths shall faint and be weary,
And the young men shall utterly fall,
³¹ But those who wait on the LORD
Shall renew their strength;
They shall mount up with wings like eagles,
They shall run and not be weary,
They shall walk and not faint. (Isaiah 40:29-31 NJKV).

Pastor, I know you have times of uncertainty, confusion, doubt and discouragement. They all come with the territory of pastoral ministry. But nothing can take the turbulence from ministry like waiting on the Lord. God gives strength to anyone who waits. He desires and delights in giving strength. It is what He does, and He has no limit to His giving.

We all can be like children on Christmas morning, with

anxious hearts ready to tear into the presents and see what we have received. But I learned a valuable lesson years ago when my wife and I started a tradition with our daughters to wait before opening any gifts until the Christmas story is read and we have prayed thanking God for His gift.

If you are too busy to wait on God, you are too busy to minister to the needs of others. Allow God to do His amazing work in your life; to serve as your Altimeter so you can stay the course. Just as waiting for the gifts on Christmas morning builds anticipation, so God will use the time of waiting in your life to build expectation toward what He is going to do, and in most cases, is already busy doing on your behalf for His glory. Just as waiting for those gifts built patience in the hearts of my children, God will build patience in your heart as you wait for His perfect timing. He will use the time of waiting to build your character and to increase His intimacy with you.

I have the following taped to the wall in a prominent place in my office to serve as a constant reminder to me:

"We're in no hurry, GOD. We're content to linger in the path sign-posted with your decisions. Who you are and

what you've done are all we'll ever want." (Isaiah 26:8 TM).

I am convinced that our failure to learn to wait on God will serve to increase the distance between us and Him. Wait my friend, wait on the Lord. Do not rush ahead to your own conclusions. If you fail to wait on Him, you will be essentially fighting without the armor of God. Do not fight naked. (See Ephesians 6:13-18)

2. Airspeed Indicator – *speed of aircraft relative to surrounding air.*

I jumped out of a plane once at the encouragement of a friend and immediately gasped for air because the surrounding air was moving by so rapidly. I had to deploy a parachute to slow my decline and keep the air from suffocating me. Many pastors are serving at such a high rate of speed they can hardly catch their breath and will surely suffocate spiritually if they do not slow down. Is this you?

APPLICATION: Sometimes it seems that the ministry we are assigned to run is actually running us. It is critical to slow the pace and avoid suffocating when the surrounding air is coming at you so quickly.

Pastoral ministry will be filled with turbulence. You cannot stop it. What you must do is learn how to manage the turbulence and use it in your favor. Free falling may provide a short lived adrenaline rush but at some point you are going to run out of room, destined to slam into the ground below. It is your responsibility to deploy the parachute and slow the decent to a manageable pace before it is too late.

Jeremiah 2:25 from The Message may help; *"Slow down. Take a deep breath. What's the hurry? Why wear yourself out? Just what are you after anyway?"*

3. Vertical Speed Indicator – *senses changes in air pressure and calculates climb and descent rate.*

APPLICATION: Some of you are in a descent rate that without adjustment, you are surely to crash; some of you are in a climb rate that without adjustment you are surely to burn out. Keeping the nose of your spiritual aircraft pointed in the right direction is critical for your spiritual health and even, to a certain degree, those around you. Best to fix your eyes on Jesus (Hebrews 12:2) before you climb too high in pride or drift too low in burn out.

I have known plenty of pastors who are burning the

candle at both ends trying to please everyone and in doing so, are not seeking to please the Lord.

The wisdom of Proverbs warns us, *"When a man's ways please the LORD, he makes even his enemies to be at peace with him."* (Proverbs 16:7).

4. Magnetic Compass – *displays the aircrafts direction in relation to magnetic north.*

APPLICATION: God does not change like shifting shadows (James 1:17). He is the same yesterday, today and forever (Hebrews 13:8). His ways never change. Keep your life magnetically attractive to His gravitational pull. He is always trying to draw you back to Him.

"You're blessed when you stay on course, walking steadily on the road revealed by God. You're blessed when you follow his directions, doing your best to find him. That's right – you don't go off on your own; you walk straight along the road he set. You, God, prescribed the right way to live; now you expect us to live it. Oh, that my steps might be steady, keeping to the course you set; Then I'd never have any regrets in comparing my life with your counsel. I thank you for

speaking straight from your heart; I learn the pattern of your righteous ways. I'm going to do what you tell me to do; don't ever walk off and leave me." (Psalm 119:1-8 TM).

5. Attitude Indicator – *shows the aircrafts relation to the horizon.*

I am sure you know plenty of people who just seem to constantly have a bad attitude. As a business owner, I have had to learn to spot attitude issues from prospective employees quickly. The Bible calls it discernment.

If we spend our time seeing the attitude problems in others, we likely will seldom, if ever, look at the attitude issues in our own life. After all, my life is really all I have control over.

APPLICATION: *"Your attitude should be the same as that of Christ Jesus"* (Philippians 2:5 NIV). As a youth pastor for many years I encouraged teenagers that "Attitude is everything" based on that verse.

As a pastor you are the pilot of the church that God has called you to serve. Please understand, I do not intend to overlook the fact that Scripture declares Jesus as the Head of the Church (Colossians 1:18; but you, pastor, are called as the leader.) If you do not keep your own attitude pointed at the horizon, you risk taking the entire church down with you, just like a pilot taking an entire plane of passengers down. Lives can be destroyed. Casualties will be far more than you can imagine. The carnage will be strewn for miles beyond what you can see now.

Unlike Jesus who *"did not consider equality with God something to be grasped,"* (Philippians 2:6 NIV), our sinful humanity is constantly looking for things to grasp to be our own God. For Adam and Eve, it was the forbidden fruit. For you and me it is the forbidden as well, often taking the shape of the pride of our heart.

Paul wrote from a prison cell when he wrote Philippians. It is amazing to think that after losing his freedom and being in chains he could pen these words, *"What happens, conduct yourselves in a manner worthy of the gospel of Christ"* (Philippians 1:27 NIV).

I dare say that whatever persecution we face will pale in comparison to what Paul and other early Church Christ followers endured. And yet we know that Paul was able to tell us, whatever happens, your attitude must align with Jesus' attitude.

I know that ministry can be defeating and tiring. I know just how easy it is to get our eyes off the prize that has called us Heavenward. But my friends, you and I are called by God Himself, the Maker of Heaven and earth, the Creator of the universe. Though what you and I face may seem insurmountable, God is our refuge and strength, truly an ever present help in our time of need (Psalm 46:1). Fix your eyes on Him. Attitude is everything!

6. Turn Indicator – *indicates rotation along the longitudinal axis.*

For years I have battled migraine headaches that are at times, completely debilitating. Often these headaches will bring extreme sensitivity to light and sound, and will also bring vertigo, complete with dizziness and feeling utterly out of balance. I would not wish these horrific spells on anyone.

APPLICATION: Pastoral ministry can bring a great deal of headache and heartache, leaving us dizzy and with a feeling of being out of balance. You risk being pulled in a myriad of different directions. Peter wrote, *"be on your guard so that you may not be carried away by the error of lawless men and fall from your secure position"*

(2 Peter 3:17 NIV). When your life is out of balance trouble will be lurking at the door.

Without careful, thoughtful attention to our spiritual conscience, we will eventually crash and burn, taking a lot of innocent people with us. It is only a matter of time. The problem with so many of us is that we fail to read, study and remain vigilant to the flight manual – this is especially troubling for men as we hate to read the directions, thinking we can figure it out on our own.

God has provided you with a flight manual, His Word. You really do not need anything else.

The problem for many pastors is they only read it in preparation to preach rather than preparation to spur themselves on to live a holy life above reproach (Titus 1:6). God gave us His Word and His call to first prepare our soul for the battle and a holy life; then to prepare the flock.

May your preaching life never surpass your praying life.

Chapter 9

Conscience and Conviction

"When wealth is lost, nothing is lost; when health is lost, something is lost; when character is lost, all is lost." –
Billy Graham

I have spent a great deal of time discussing point one.

1. Conscience is an internal spiritual gyroscope that integrates to one's value system.

Now let us look at the remaining four points.

2. Conscience is aligning our thoughts with God's Word.

Paul said, *"I die every day"* (1 Corinthians 15:31)!

Paul also wrote, *"I discipline my body and keep it under control, lest after preaching to others I myself should be disqualified"* (1 Corinthians 9:27).

We need discipline ourselves rather than have the hand of God discipline us.

Consider the words of the Psalmist, *"Delight yourself in the LORD, and he will give you the desires of your heart."* (Psalm 37:4).

God does not promise to give us whatever our sinful hearts can conceive. He does, however, pledge to give us the desires of our heart once we have delighted ourselves in Him. Consider the words, *"give you,"* in Psalm 37:4 as *"plant in you."* By His amazing grace, God will plant in us the desires He wants our hearts to have when we delight ourselves in Him. We must remain open to His planting as His will relates to us from His Word, not from our sinful, selfish, fleshly desires. We must keep the soil of our heart plowed and ready to receive the planting of the seed that God desires into our heart.

Matthew Henry says of this verse, *"We must make God our heart's delight and then we shall have our heart's desire."*[1]

3. Conscience must be subordinate to God's Word.

Amos poses an important question, *"Do two walk together unless they have agreed to do so"* (Amos 3:3 NIV)?

The Psalmist proclaimed that God's Word is a lamp unto our feet and a light unto our path (Psalm 119:105). If you are going to walk in fellowship with Him, you must agree to walk as He directs.

What is the difference between *light* and *lamp*? Consider the *light* of God's Word as you walk each step, perhaps a few inches at a time, and the *lamp* as you gaze down the trail to what is ahead, further down the path. The light will illuminate directly in front of you while the lamp will show you clearly what is coming your way from a distance. God has thought of everything – the near and the far away; and He is providing clear illumination for it all.

4. Conscience is what convicts us when we willfully transgress God's Word.

A simple definition of sin could be, "A willful transgression against the known will of God."

"For whatever does not proceed from faith is sin." (Romans 14:23). It is impossible to please God without faith (Hebrews 11:6), and it is one's faith that grounds us to God's promises, providing us with the ability to avoid sinful behavior.

Transgressions most often occur as a result of our lack of faith. When our faith is lacking, temptation is crouched at the door ready to leap in and attack. Christ followers are called to, *"walk by faith, not by sight."* (2 Corinthians 5:7). When we walk merely by the seen and ignore the unseen, we are failing to walk in faith and therefore sin against God and invite more temptation our way. God will light the way, but still we are to walk by faith.

The enemy of God stands in direction opposition to faith.

5. Conscience can be seared by sin.

1 Timothy 4, *"The Spirit clearly says that in latter times some will abandon the faith and follow deceiving spirits and things taught by demons. Such teachings come through hypocritical liars, whose consciences have been seared as with a hot iron."* (1 Timothy 4:1-2 NIV).

In my sin, though my conscience bothered me, I hid my thoughts away until they became actions that had to be hidden away.

Sin is always birthed in our thoughts, traveling to our heart into our actions.

Sin will always cause a sense of guilt for the born again.

People with a seared conscience are always tempted to think more highly of themselves than they ought.

Richard Dortch wrote, *"Once our reputation grows among the circles in which we live, travel, work, or worship, that distinction begins to take on a life of its own. A certain synergy develops that allows us to think more highly of ourselves than is safe to do."* [2]

Partly because of the accolades of others, my conscience could no longer hear the truth. That is not to say that we should not speak positively to others, nor is it meant to identify me as a victim. Rather my life was out of focus with the will of God. The still small voice of Holy Spirit was drowned out by my own allowance of the words spoken by man to invade my spirit. It is simply too easy to magnify the compliments and minimize the complaints.

Numeric growth can be intoxicating and can blind us to the true growth of self and those around us that God so desperately desires for us. I was allured by the lie that my strength, confidence and charisma was producing growth. I had forgotten the Lord, which is the first step to failure.

In Hosea, God lays out the recipe for disaster that caused Israel's downfall.

"I cared for you in the desert in the land of burning heat. When I fed them, they were satisfied; when they were satisfied, they became proud; then they forgot me." (Hosea 13:5-6 NIV).

Again, I say, that is why the Bible says, *"give me neither poverty nor riches, but give me only my daily bread. Otherwise, I may have too much and disown you and say, 'Who is the LORD?' Or I may become poor and steal, and so dishonor the name of my God."* (Proverbs 30:8-9 NIV).

Notice that in Hosea the care of the Lord was first trumped by the people becoming satisfied, then followed by pride until they forgot Him and what He had done for them.

Richard Dortch, *"When arrogance about our own reputation and integrity dominates our life, then we get out of sync and wrong decisions are inevitable."* [3]

Tom Peters says, *"There is no such thing as a minor lapse in integrity."* [4]

Robert Dortch, *"Truth cannot be selective. This is how integrity is lost."* He goes on, *"Selective integrity is ... doing evil and expecting good to come from it."* [5]

The cause of moral failure for many pastors is the idea that God has given them gifts, so they are to run with their giftedness devoid of a remaining sense of God's moment-by-moment presence being required. Too many pastors are serving the Lord without the presence of Holy Spirit.

That is why I have often said that prayer is to the body of Christ what breath is for the human body. In 1997, Jim Cymbala wrote, *"the prayer meeting will be the barometer of our church"* [6] as he spoke of the renewed sense that God had spoken to him directly about the need for prayer to be the centerpiece in order to have any success in the fledgling inner-city church God had called him to, the Brooklyn Tabernacle.

The church can do nothing of lasting value devoid of the summoned presence of Holy Spirit.

Charles Spurgeon would also write, *"The condition of the church may be very accurately gauged by its prayer meetings."* [7] Truly, our only hope for lasting, viable ministry is in prayer, both privately in our prayer closet, and corporately as the body of Jesus Christ. Perhaps the greatest challenge of the local church pastor today is finding a group of people, albeit a small group, that is willing to commit to faithful, regular, fervent corporate prayer.

E. M. Bounds wrote, *"The neglect of prayer is the fearful token of dead spiritual desires. The soul has turned away from God when desire after him no longer presses it into the closet. There can be no true praying without desire."*[8]

"No man is greater than his prayer life. The pastor who is not praying is playing; the people who are not praying are straying. The pulpit can be a shop window to display one's talents; the prayer closet allows no showing off."
– Leonard Ravenhill

If you desire to have your conscience be your guide, you

had better immerse your conscience in the Word of God and remain sensitive to the prompting of Holy Spirit.

Chapter 10

Culture & Church

"There are three persons living in each of us: the one we think we are, the one other people think we are, and the one God knows we are."
– Leonard Ravenhill, Why Revival Tarries

Culture

The term "Christian" is often misused as an adverb or adjective, as for "Christian music" or "Christian culture." One is left to wonder how inanimate objects like music and culture can *be* Christian. And they would not be if it were not for the people involved in the music and the culture. But the word "Christian" is a noun used to describe a specific group of people. The Bible has Greek cultures and Jewish cultures, but not Christian cultures. Christianity is a belief that is intended to inform and inspire and provoke change on certain cultural groups.

Our world views "Christian" as a set of actions that virtually anyone can adapt without claiming that those actions come from God or His Word. The culture puts emphasis on the *way* we express rather than *what* we express. Christianity is all about "the what" and "the Who" rather than "the way" or "the method." Christianity is not defined as methodology, rather by action and service; and the action and service in Christianity revolves around Jesus Christ at its center. In other words, Christianity ceases to exist when devoid of the personal presence of the Person, Jesus the Christ.

Romans 12:2, *"Do not conform any longer to the pattern of this world, but be transformed by the renewing of your mind"* (NIV). "**Pattern** of this world" are the customs, methods or principles of the world, which involves the way the world, or culture, reacts and responses to certain events.

Notice the phrase "any longer" in the above-mentioned verse. God's Word is mandating that we must stop conforming any longer to the patterns that are opposite to the transformational power that comes through the biblical, spiritual renewal of one's mind. There is a way out, a way back to God. What we have once lived for we can die to. The way it has been is not the way it has to remain. We can be transformed if we cease to conform.

John 15:19, *"If you belonged to the world, it would love you as its own. As it is, you do not belong to the world, but I have chosen you out of the world"* (NIV).

When the call of Christians is to be *in the world but not of the world*, it has become even difficult to distinguish in many cases the difference between many pastors because of their behavior, dress and personal choices. This may be a clear indication that the influence of the culture is greater on the church than the influence of the church on the culture.

The Bible is clear that there must be a distinction between the values of the world and the values of God's children, the church of the living God. 1 John is a prime example of God's expectations of His church; *"Do not love the world or the things in the world. If anyone loves the world, the love of the Father is not in him. For all that is in the world – the desires of the flesh and the desires of the eyes and pride of life – is not from the Father but is from the world. And the world is passing away along with its desires, but whoever does the will of God abides forever"* (1 John 2:15-17).

John Wesley said, "The world is my parish." Unfortunately, many of us would admit that the world is **in** our parish. God's call is for us to be different, peculiar to the culture so as to stand out in distinction to what the world is and offers. 1 Peter 2:11 says that we are *"aliens and strangers"* in this world, and we must *"abstain from fleshly lusts, which wage war against the soul"* (1 Peter 2:11 NASB).

Let me be clear: I do think pastors should have their finger on the pulse of the culture, but their mind on the Word of God and how It can influence and win the culture.

Which brings us to the next arena of accepted wrongdoing. The Church.

Church

"I count him braver who overcomes his desires than him who conquers his enemies, for the hardest victory is over self." – Aristotle

I was worship leader years ago in a church in our area when one day following worship a small boy approached me and asked, "Who owns the church?" I quickly asked the boy, "What do you mean?" He replied, "Who is the owner of this church? Is Pastor Jeff the owner?"

Many of us think we own the church. It is clear when we say things like, "My church." Not to mention the many arguments church attendees have engaged in over everything from the color of the nursery walls to the color of carpet in the sanctuary. We think that everything is our responsibility and so we work ourselves into believing (conscience) that we must give people what they want (culture) in order for them to continue to come (to church). It is evangelism by manipulation. The church is the one being manipulated.

Jesus told Peter, *"And I tell you that you are Peter, and on this rock I will build my church, and the gates of hades will not overcome it"* (Matthew 16:18 NIV).

Jesus' words come following Peter's confession that Jesus is, *"the Christ, the Son of the living God."* (Matthew 16:16 NIV).

God will build His Church with or without you. And quite honestly, He may have an easier time doing so without some of you unless you adjust the sails and set a new course in the direction of a holy God. Those who parade around proudly that they are above temptation eventually become demeaning and overbearing to members of the congregation, even the culture, overlooking the desire to serve and what each can contribute to the work of the Lord. The enemy will woo us into a sense that we are the cause of whatever growth the church enjoys, and the church just would not survive without us.

What is the *"rock"* that Jesus spoke of? Is it Peter's faith? Is it Peter's confession? Is it Jesus Himself?

Catholicism teaches that Peter is the rock because, as any devout Catholic will tell you, Peter went to Rome and became the first Pope. But Jesus would tell Peter *"Get behind me, Satan! You are a hindrance to me"* (Matthew 16:23), and Peter would deny Jesus three times before His crucifixion (Matthew 26:69-75). Clearly Jesus did not build His Church on Peter, and Jesus is not referring to Peter as "the rock."

The rock that He was going to build His Church on was the rock bed of Peter's confession. Jesus used two different words, "Peter," or "Petra," which means stone, and rock. So, Jesus was saying, "You are a stone, Peter. I will build my Church on the truth of your confession. Thus, it is on the bedrock truth that came from Peter's lips that Jesus would build His Church on; not on a person.

So, Pastor, you are a stone, but Jesus wants His church built on the rock, not on stones. He can build His church through you when you recognize the value of your confession as it stands against eternity. When you recognize your confession is a response to God's invitation, you become all the more humble. The first four words from Rick Warren's classic book seem to ring so clear, "It's not about you." [1] The creation, construction and sustaining of God's church has never been about us, it is about our place in the world as we recognize His greatest, and with awe, surrender to His call to preach the Word.

God has never intended that His Church be thought of as buildings, rather, about people of faith, loving and serving God, and confessing their need for Him, every moment of every day.

Corinthians says, *"Do you not know that you are God's temple and that God's Spirit dwells in you? If anyone destroys God's temple, God will destroy him. For God's temple is holy, and you are that temple"* (1 Corinthians 3:16-17).

I can be the greatest fan and biggest cheerleader of the pastor. But let me tell you this, if you are living with one foot in the Bible and one foot in sin, you have lost the privilege and ability to lead. You cannot build God's Church, no matter how hard you try; it cannot be done by man. Only Jesus will build His Church on the brokenness and confession of His children. You may have the charisma to put a lot of bodies in the building, but the spiritual depth will be shallow at best, and you will be lacking the spiritual anointing needed to lead God's people effectively.

Perhaps what the church needs is not more faith, but *deeper* faith. Not more faith in our own abilities, but deeper faith that God will build His church. It was Frank Viola who is credited as saying, "Modern Christianity is ten miles wide and one inch deep." God help us to be the church and allow God to have His way with us as we confess our need for more of Him.

John 3:30, *"He must increase, but I must decrease."*

My downfall

My focus became, and ultimately one of my sins was, that I was trying to build the church. After all it was my education and degrees, charisma, calling on visitors, coming up with flashy PowerPoint slides and creative illustrations that was causing numerical growth in the church – at least that became how I saw it. I had bought the sales pitch to attend as many church growth seminars as possible and had accepted the mantle of responsibility for that growth. Let us not forget, that every year I would have to give a report in front of my peers and denominational leaders for the growth or decline of both the attendance and finances. Misunderstanding what the church was really all about became a part of my downfall.

I do not want to give the impression that my fall was the church's blame. It was my misdirected understanding of my role and my unwillingness to see the danger signs that became the catalyst for my demise. Let me encourage you to consider attending fewer church growth seminars and calling more prayer meetings.

Let me add one more element.

Chapter 11

To Resend or not to Rescind

"God's gifts and God's call are under full warranty –
never canceled, never rescinded"
Romans 11:29 TM

I was talking on the cell phone in my car with a friend and accountability partner on an evening in May 2019 and as sometimes happens, the call dropped. I had lost the connection with my friend. When I looked down at my cell phone, I saw the words, "Call failure." It stopped me in my tracks mental. Never before had I seen those words and thought this, but I was faced with my own call failure as a pastor. Even after all these years since my fall, it still sometimes causes me to pause and consider my life, my actions; but more importantly, the inescapable power and depth of God's grace and call.

You see, just like my cell phone dropped the call with my friend, I had dropped my call from God with my Friend; His name is Jesus. But just as I reconnected with my friend on the cell phone later as we re-established our connection, I have reconnected with my Friend, Jesus and we have re-established our connection, and my call.

Romans says, *"God's gifts and call are irrevocable"* (Roman 11:29 NIV).

If God has truly called you, He will not revoke that call even though we stray sometimes from Him. The power of the initial sanctification of our hearts to God is the same power He uses to re-establish us in our walk and even in our ministry. There is a great deal of work that He expects on our end. The Apostle Paul said we should *"work out your own salvation with fear and trembling"* (Philippians 2:12).

As John Eldredge says, *"when you neglect the sanctifying of the heart, you set yourself up for a fall."* [1] God did not intend for Paul to say that we should "work **for** our own salvation," that would remove the role that God's grace has in reaching us. But God does expect us to be vigilantly involved in our own spiritual growth by

174

keeping ourselves in Him.

I have learned that not only can God restore a repentant heart back to right relationship with Him, He can restore the call of a fallen pastor who is sincerely repentant and seeks to honor Him. In fact, God can even restore our reputation if we are willing to allow truth and repentance to collide and understand that reputation rebuilding can take a great deal of time.

On October 31, 1517, Martin Luther nailed his 95 theses to the door of the Wittenberg Church. The very first of those theses reads, "Our Lord and Master Jesus Christ, in saying, 'Repent ye, etc.' intended that the whole life of his believers on earth should be a constant penance."

Repentance is not just for people coming to Christ for the first time as sinners in need of a Savior, repentance is perpetual. Repentance is a continual work for all of us, the greater we see our Savior, the greater we see our sin. Repentance is perpetual.

In order to keep your cell phone from dropping calls you have to reset it or get closer to the cell tower. It may be time that you reset some things in your life before you drop your calling from God and suffer the horrific consequences. It may be time for you to draw near to "the strong tower" (Proverbs 18:10) and re-establish your connection.

If God has truly called you, He will not rescind that call. He will not allow you to live in flagrant disobedience and continue to preach. So, one of two things will happen:

1. You will leave the sinful behavior and restore your soul to God through true, biblical repentance. You will walk in your calling with more anointing than ever before.

2. You will continue living a duplicitous life and risk losing everything. You will remain unrepentant and have no anointing.

You cannot live a life of duplicity and expect to receive the Lord's anointing. You must resist the temptation, even for a moment, and press into God's presence and His best for you.

The enemy uses three areas to increase temptation in our lives, especially when it comes to sexual sin.
1. Isolation
2. Boredom

3. Exhaustion

Allow me to offer a brief explanation of each.

Isolation. Men especially have a difficult time with friendships and accountability. It is in times of isolation that the enemy can be so relentless. Remember that Jesus was alone in the desert when the enemy tempted Him so fiercely.

Proverbs declares, *"Whoever isolates himself seeks his own desire; he breaks out against all sound judgment"* (Proverbs 18:1). When feeling tempted, the worst thing we can do is isolate ourselves, because it is in isolation we are tempted all the more. God never called us to fight the good fight solo.

In 1 Timothy 6:12 Paul reminded young Timothy, *"Fight the good fight of the faith. Take hold of the eternal life to which you were called when you made your good confession in the presence of many witnesses."*

We do not serve and fight alone, rather in a presence of witnesses. Though the enemy does not want us to seek accountability or spiritual partnership with other like-minded believers, it becomes one of our greatest tools as

Christ followers to seek out partners we are willing to give permission to hold us accountable. I have had several men as accountability partners over the years and faced tough questions. You must be willing to allow people to ask you hard questions regarding schedule and your time spent alone. If you fail to allow people the privilege of holding you accountable, you risk falling for one of the oldest tricks of the devil – "I can do this on my own and I'll be fine."

Two fears can drive us to isolation:

1. Fear of being caught and ashamed to talk about it.
2. Fear of being judged and cast out.

Boredom. Another area the enemy will exploit to bring temptation is boredom. It has been said, *"An idle mind is the devil's playground."*

Socrates said, *"Beware the barrenness of a busy life."* Sometimes even the routine and mundane can become boring and open us up for temptation.

While many pastors are extremely busy with appointments, study and counseling, there are definitely down times when the enemy is poised and ready to bring temptation right to your doorstep. It may even be *during* times of appointments, study and counseling that the enemy brings vicious temptation. Nothing good ever comes from boredom. An unchecked mind is a runaway mind. I have found it helpful to "busy" myself with scripture memorization as ammunition so that when I am tempted, I can, like Jesus, quote Scripture to my adversary. Allow the brain to idle for too long will eventually invite thoughts that are ungodly. Remember, *"we wrestle not against flesh and blood, but against principalities, against powers, against the rulers of the darkness of this world, against spiritual wickedness in high places"* (Ephesians 6:12 KJV).

This does not mean that we have to maintain a ultra-busy lifestyle without breaks or down times; God expects us to honor and celebrate the Sabbath and we need periodic extended times away from our ministry. Do not be fooled into thinking that you will not be tempted when your mind is idle.

Exhaustion. Exhaustion can be another arena in which the enemy delights to use to tempt us. There is a fine line between boredom and exhaustion, but both can provide opportunity for the enemy to temp us. I find comfort in Paul's words in Galatians, *"So let's not allow ourselves to get fatigued doing good. At the right time we will harvest a good crop if we don't give up or quit"* (Galatians 6:9 TM).

As a pastor, I am tempted to feel like I am on the clock 24/7/365, having to answer the phone whenever it rings, having to drop what I am doing whenever anyone drops by or calls no matter the time of day or the activity I am involved in. The ego has a way of fooling us into thinking that we are more important than we really are. If you do not care for yourself first in the area of rest, you will not only be failing yourself, but also those around you. Carve out intentional times of rest and be sure to observe a Sabbath's rest every week. It is sinful not to!

I find it helpful to find secluded places that I can go to spend limited time alone in God's Word and in prayer. If you are missing times like that, you are setting yourself up for failure. Even Jesus had to get away from crowds from time to time.

Mark 1 records, *"And rising very early in the morning, while it was still dark, he departed and went out to a desolate place, and there he prayed"* (Mark 1:35).

Luke 5 says that *"Jesus often withdrew to lonely places*

and prayed. " (Luke 5:16 NIV).

When He was *"in anguish, he prayed more earnestly, and his sweat was like drops of blood"* (Luke 22:44 NIV).

If Jesus could not go it alone, what makes you think you can? Perhaps pride and idolatry?

Set aside pride, you must abide.

Jesus says in John, *"If you abide in me, and my words abide in you, ask whatever you wish, and it will be done for you. By this my Father is glorified, that you bear much fruit, and so prove to be my disciples"* (John 15:7-8).

Imagine your house is your spiritual life and you diligently work to keep only the rooms clean that you plan to allow the Lord into. The problem is that sin does not exist in just one room; sin will cut off the power supply completely.

James said, *"whoever keeps the whole law but fails in one point has become guilty of all of it"* (James 2:10).

In 2011 tornadoes ravished North Alabama leaving our city without power for five days. Sin does not just affect one area of your life; it will leave your whole being without power.

Are all sins the same?

I have heard many people, even pastors, claim that all sins are the same in the eyes of God. While it is true we are all sinners in need of a Savior (Romans 3:23), I cannot agree that all sins are equal, bearing the same consequences. If you think all sins are equal, please show me a city that God destroyed because of gossip. How about cursing? Both gossip and cursing are sins, but God destroyed Sodom and Gomora because of the sexual sin of the people.

If you need more proof, just take a look at Romans 1 and see what it has to say about those who *"exchanged the truth of God for a lie, and worshiped and served created things rather than the Creator – who is forever praised"* (Romans 1:25 NIV).

Humility vs. Humiliation:

"A proud man is always looking down on things and people; and, of course, as long as you are looking down, you cannot see something that is above you."

– C. S. Lewis, Mere Christianity

One of the most Christ-like men I ever knew I first met when I was a backward 15-year-old that started attending church to date a girl. This man would have tremendous influence in my life. He was recently diagnosed with stage four cancer. I went to see my friend twice before the cancer quickly claimed his life. I shared with him how he had been such an inspiration to so many and particularly to me over the last 40 years. His tearful response caught me off guard but speaks so appropriately to what it means to be humble. He said, "Keith, I was just living." He had not lived his life to be seen by others, but to see the glory of God come alive *in* others.

Really what it comes down to is we humble ourselves before the Lord. I have found few ever really understand what that means.

For many years I prayed that God would humble me, over and over and over again I prayed for God to remove my pride and make me humble; until I read and understood James and Peter that said, *"Humble yourselves before the Lord"* (James 4:10; 1 Peter 5:6). It was as if God was pushing the argument back across the table to me and saying, "Humility really is up to you.

When you humble yourself, I will have something I can work with."

Richard Dortch found *"As the ministry at PTL began to grow rapidly, my confidence in my own integrity blurred my need for humility before the Lord."* [2]

Humility and *humiliation* are from the same root word, yet they could not be farther apart in biblical meaning and understanding.

Humility is an inward work that causes in us an inner surrender and will be evidenced by our outward behavior, while *humiliation* is outward work and can be thrust upon us by someone else that can cause inward turmoil.

Humility is our surrender before the Lord. The proud fall and fail, but the humble are lifted up by God Himself for His own glory. It has long been my contention that humility is the only biblical attribute that once claimed, is lost. How foolish does it sound to hear someone say, "I am humble." The emphasis, after-all, is on "I," and is the antithesis to humility.

A young teenager in a youth ministry I led years ago told me, "Keith, God has given me the gift of humility; and

I'm proud of it." It would be funny except it is so true. Often times we become prideful of, yes, even our self-imposed, false humility. Pride is the antithesis of humility. It is therefore impossible to be proud of being humble. That is idolatry.

I was sharing the lesson of humility with a group of youth one evening and to illustrate the point, I said, "I cannot humble any of you, but I could humiliate any of you." One young man mouthed to me, "Bring it on" to me. Humility cannot be mocked. Some years later that same young man became entrapped in disgusting, sinful behavior, all because he remained prideful and refused to heed the warning and humble himself before the Lord.

The story is told of a man who complained to a museum curator that he could not see Jesus' face on the statue of Him hanging on the cross because Jesus' head was drooped down too far. Finally, the museum curator said, "Sir, in order to see Jesus' face, you must bend down in front of Him and look up."

That my friends is the greatest example I know of how we must humble ourselves in order to see Jesus' face. We must bend down before Him and look up. Better to humble oneself before the Lord from one's heart before humiliation is brought before you from the outside.

Malachi says, *"For the lips of a priest should guard knowledge, and people should seek instruction from his mouth, for he is the messenger of the LORD of hosts. But you have turned aside from the way. You have caused many to stumble by your instruction. You have corrupted the covenant of Levi, says the LORD of hosts, and so I make you despised and abased before all the people, inasmuch as you do not keep my ways but have shown partiality in your instruction"* (Malachi 2:7-9).

Whether you are a professed fan of southern gospel music or not, I think you will find that the lyrics to The Cathedrals Quartet song, Sin Will Take You Farther, to be quite convicting.

Sin Will Take You Farther – The Cathedrals Quartet [3]

Sin will take you farther than you wanna go
Slowly but wholly taking control
Sin will leave you longer than you wanna stay
Sin will cost you far more than you wanna pay

Where Were You When He Called Your Name?

I was a young Corporal in the Army at the end of my brief enlistment and was trying to discern what to do with my life. At 21 years old I had only known my experience in fast food (my first and only job before the Army), and the short stint I spent serving my country. Now what?

The answer came to me as uniquely as perhaps your call did. My decision to either reenlist or exit the military had to be made – I was at the make or break point and had to make a decision; a decision that would likely have altered the rest of my life; stay in the Army and consider a career, or get out and perhaps go back into fast food management.

I was helping a friend work on a car on a hot summer day in Fayetteville, North Carolina and as clearly as I can remember, I felt the Lord say to my spirit, "You are going to move to Nashville, go to college and get a degree in ministry." No altar. No pastoral counsel. No deep questioning and prodding from a pastor. No family to embrace. Just a quiet moment with God Himself as I leaned over the fender and under the hood of that old car. I called my wife and told her the news, and that was what sent us on the journey of many years serving God in several churches across the country.

I go back to that moment often, especially when I am

tempted to doubt my call and ability. God has stamped that call in my mind so I will never forget that He called me, not the church, not my wife, not a pastor; God called me. My call is a private experience I shared only with the Creator of the universe in that moment of complete uncertainty, and yet with complete honesty and surrender, seeking to do whatever God would have me to do. Of course, now, in the offering of my gifts to the church, I share my call with the body of Christ in the form of recognizing and using my spiritual gifts for His glory.

It would do you well to recount your call and allow God to remind you that the work you are involved in is His work first and foremost. He is using you as a vessel of love and encouragement in this world. Forgetting that truth will likely be the first step in drifting from His presence.

I, like Paul, *"am sure of this, that he who began a good work in you will bring it to completion at the day of Jesus Christ"* (Philippians 1:6).

The truth is, rarely do Christians run from their values; most often we drift from them. It is a slow, methodical drift that almost has us entranced while we fix our eyes on things other than God. For many of us, we aren't even aware that we are drifting. For me, it was numerical growth and that is where I found my value as a pastor. I was a performer trying to give a better performance from week to week than I had given before.

Does that sound familiar? If you were to be completely honest will yourself, would you say the same is true for you?

The devil is a thief and a liar, but he really cannot take anything from you that you are not willing to let him have. The problem is that many of us are asleep at the wheel of our own life, drifting from point to point, not realizing the impact of even the smallest encounters and moments.

Hebrews 2:1 says, *"we must pay much closer attention to what we have heard, lest we drift away from it."*

It is time to pay attention.

Broken, Broke and Brought Back

Chapter 12

Broken

"It is in our darkest moments that we must focus to see the light." – Aristotle

Richard Dortch illustrates in his book, *Losing It All & Finding Yourself*, that it took Joseph and Mary three times as long to find Jesus than it took to lose him. He says he learned that, "It usually takes us much longer to regain what we have lost than it took for us to lose it in the first place." [1] How true.

One counselor told us that it typically takes as long to recover for the offended spouse than it did for the offender to enter the illicit relationship and get caught. Richard points out that because Mary had lost Jesus once, she had to have a much better memory in order to never lose him again; and, he points out that Jesus was lost in the temple, and, *"we can lose Jesus in the temple*

– the place of our most spiritual activity." [2] He then says, *"To find Him, we must go back to the place where we lost Him."*

Two of the greatest lies of the devil are with enough effort, you can accomplish the law; and with enough sin you can undo grace.

But here is the truth:
- God cannot love you any more than He already does. He loves you with an everlasting love (Jeremiah 31:3).

- God cannot love you any less than He already does. Nothing can separate us from His love (Romans 8:38-39).

When an expensive vase falls from the mantle and shatters on the hearth, it cannot be repaired to "like new" condition; it will forever be known as broken, shattered, un-useable. If the pieces are big enough, you may be able to glue it back together into some semblance of what it once was, but it will forever be changed and perhaps never to be appreciated like it was before.

That is how many fallen pastors feel; that they have no chance at being used again for the glory of the Lord; that they are shattered, un-useable, suffering from too much shame to ever try to put the pieces back together and try again.

Kintsugi

Kintsugi is an ancient Japanese art form whereby cracked or broken pottery is repaired using gold to fill in the crevices and cracks making the piece not only unique, but even more valuable than it was before the breakage. Rather than trying to hide the imperfection, Kintsugi seeks to highlight the imperfections and build on the history of the piece and expand its value.

God has no plan B. When we fall or fail; when we are broken and feel completely un-useable, He takes us right where we are and builds on our imperfections when we repent and turn from our sin. He does not create a "lesser plan" than the one He had before. Because of His presence in our lives and filling in the crevices, we become even more valuable to the work of Christ in the world, provided we are, again, submitting to His authority in our lives. We are all cracked pots, finding our true value when we submit to the Master's refining hand and allow the things the enemy meant for harm, to be used for God's glory.

Do not let the enemy tell you that because of a failure you are worthless. God sees you and uses you as a unique piece that He can make even more valuable to His kingdom work than ever before. You are *Kintsugi*. Do not attempt to become something you are not. Do not attempt to hide what you really are and are becoming, by the grace and work of Almighty God. Refuse to accept the labels of failure placed on you by others.

Mark Batterson wrote, "Please don't let anyone name you except God. You are not the labels people put on you. You are who God says you are!" [3]

IP Address

Speaking of uniqueness, it is likely that you possess at least one computer. Depending on where you live in the world, if you do not own a computer, you are in the minority of people who can engage in the digital world. Consider the unique IP address of every single computer on the planet.

IP stands for *Internet Protocol*. Every computer that accesses the internet is given a unique identity code. For ease of understanding, allow me to give a simple list of facts about IP addresses:

- IP addresses act like mailing addresses so locations on the internet can receive and send information to your device.
- IP addresses are unique to every device.
- IP addresses are assigned by internet providers.
- IP addresses can change if changes occur (i.e. accessing the internet from a different location, etc.)

Your spiritual IP address involves your *Identity* and your *Purpose*. Let us consider the spiritual IP, your *Identifying Purpose*. In short, who you are and why you exist defines your giftedness and uniqueness, and God is committed to assigning those things to each of us. You are so important to Him that He does not leave those assignments up to anyone else. Only God assigns us our spiritual IP address. So, think about this:

1. You are unique to God; He has assigned you a unique spiritual address to communicate His truths to you. He can communicate specifically to you regardless of what everyone else hears.

2. God has created you uniquely different than anyone else who has ever lived. Of the billions of fingerprints assigned by God to human beings for the past 6,000

years, there have never been another set that matches yours. The same unique spiritual giftedness belongs to you.

3. God assigns values and addresses, no one else. Too often we allow the world to dictate our value because of perception or mistakes – *labels*. God never loses hope in us. He values you! Highly!

4. Your address can change when you wander to other locations and communication with God becomes scrambled.

If you are a fallen pastor, you are still as wonderfully unique as you were the day God formed you in your mother's womb. Falling from grace does not mean you have necessarily lost the call of God on your life. You can be restored, and the ministry you have moving forward can be more effective and produce more fruit than ever before.

Your IP address may have changed, but you can still be in God's will.

God has no plan B. Wherever you find yourself right now with a repentant heart, is God's plan A for you. Do not allow the enemy to rob you of the blessing of serving

God with the gifts you have. God is speaking *kintsugi* over you!

Remember, horses, by nature, are wild animals. They must be trained to submit to the leading and instruction of the rider, their master. The process is lengthy and sometimes difficult, but when the horse if fully broken, it will submit to the hand of its master and can be enjoyed by many.

Rather than seeing your life as broken like a vase and unusable, see your life as broken like a horse, ready to submit to the authority of the Master, Jesus Christ.

Your past *wandering* and *sin* must not define your present *worship* and *service*. You can be broken and still be useable, perhaps now more than ever before, if you are fully submitted to the Master.

Broken, Broke and Brought Back

Conclusion

"God presents the Sabbath rest as a shelter we can enter. (Hebrews 4:1-11)." – Charles Swindoll

No matter the time you spend thinking about going to the gym and lifting weights, it will never happen until you actually do it. The same is true for our waiting on the Lord. Psalms instructs us, *"Be still and know that I am God."* (Psalm 46:10).

It has long been my contention that Christians need more *wait* training. The busyness of life draws us in to a pace causing us to forget God, ignore the needs of others, and even is the cause of many physical ailments we see in our society. Our prayer life is one of the greatest examples of us taking the reins of our out of control life, and slowing it down.

Leonard Ravenhill is right, *no man is greater than his prayer life. No church is greater than its prayer life.* It is sadly the prayer life of the modern church that is sorely lacking, in need of rediscovering the prayer passion of our brothers and sisters who have gone before. We seem to have become too hip and cool for prayer meetings and if we even bother with prayer, it is a passing theme at best in most of our churches. We prefer the solo prayer life devoid of any accountability or agreement. Simply put, we lack the Acts 2 commitment in prayer of the New Testament Church.

There is a spirit of apathy among our society. Generation after generation drifts further from the precepts of God's Word, and we see the drift in the deterioration in our society in every aspect: business, education, retail, even in our homes and, yes, even in our churches.

Busy schedules and misplaced priorities are among the causes of the condition in which the modern day church finds herself. Though we have an abundance of worldly possessions, *discouragement*, *despair* and *distance* from God seems to be ever increasing in our personal lives and our homes. Just as the audience that the book of Romans was written to, we have exchanged the truth of God for a lie, and worship and serve created things rather than the Creator (Romans 1:25).

Just as God had given Paul's audience over to their sinful desires, it seems the same has happened to us. We are hard pressed to find modern day preachers who seem to understand the reality of what is happening and have enough conviction to speak the truth.

Jesus' disciples did **not** say, "Teach us to preach." They asked, *"Teach us to pray"* (Luke 11:1 NIV). We are not going to move a generation to God except by a Holy Ghost revival through fervent prayer, led by men and women of God, who desire to seek God more than anything else in their lives.

We have plenty of college and seminary degrees, plenty of doctorates and knowledge; what we need is application of the Word of God; application of what we already know. We have become good *organizers of programs* rather than *agonizers in prayer*. It is time we stop organizing and start agonizing! We must revive the art of waiting on the Lord in fervent prayer.

When Jesus' disciples asked Him to teach them to pray, He did just that. The illustration that follows is of greater importance than the prayer itself. You cannot reach God by simply reciting words; you cannot reach God even because He is your friend. You can only reach God through the *persistence* of prayer (Luke 11:8).

Lack of persistence is like someone who knocks on a door and walks away, verses someone who will not stop knocking until the door is opened. Jesus' intent in teaching The Lord's Prayer is that we would shamelessly persist in approaching God's throne, not with selfish motives, but with pure motives, seeking the will of Father. Unfortunately, we too often give up after mere seconds of waiting at the door.

So many preachers have degrees on the walls of their offices and certificates declaring they are ordained to preach the Word of God. Certificates of ordination can be downloaded from the internet. I do not mean to lessen the call or effect of ordination, rather to make a point: our calling has to be more passionate.

Many know the Word of God, yet do not know the God of the Word, Whom can only be found in persistent prayer, not degrees or certificates. You may have proof you are a preacher, but is there proof you are passionate about God?

Peter and John were dragged before Annas, the high priest for preaching that salvation comes through the name of the resurrected Jesus Christ. Though Peter and John had no degrees or formal training, it was because of their testimony the council knew *"these men had been with Jesus"* (Acts 4:13 NIV).

Let me ask you this question pastor, if your seminary

degrees and preaching certificates were stripped from your walls, would there be enough evidence in your life that people would know you had been with Jesus?

You may be a tremendous preacher, pulpiteer, writer, theologian; but if you have not been with Jesus, you are sorely lacking the intimacy you so need personally, and your congregation so needs to see in you.

Jesus was the greatest preacher ever to live, preaching sermons that still shape societies to this day, and yet, when given an opportunity to ask something of Him, the men closest to Him did not ask Him to teach them how to preach, but they asked Him to teach them how to pray.

Our churches have heard enough sermons, what they need is to see one in the life of their shepherd. It is not just secular society that is rejecting Christianity, it seems the church is rejecting Christianity.

We no longer believe with enough passion that persistence in prayer is the call of Father to rescue us from ourselves. We have become content to reduce our passion for Christ to flashy songs and sermons, dress and dance; and the whole time providing no evidence we have even been with Jesus (see Acts 4:13). We are not in need of more preaching; we are in need of more passion. We are in need of fervent prayer.

Our society is drowning in theological knowledge, yet greatly lacking a thirst for righteousness.

Leonard Ravenhill said, *"Preaching, we stand before man on behalf of God; praying we stand before God on behalf of man."*

Ravenhill also said, *"A man who is intimate with God will never be intimidated by men."*

We, like Peter, James and John, have been found sleeping while Jesus is praying. We have failed to keep watch with Jesus in prayer, and we have become content to keep watch over numbers in attendance and in the money in the offering. If the numbers go down, our anxiety goes up, and only then do we seem to care enough about prayer to enlist God's help.

Deuteronomy 23:21-23, *"If you make a vow to the LORD your God, you shall not delay fulfilling it, for the LORD your God will surely require it of you, and you will be guilty of sin. But if you refrain from vowing, you will not be guilty of sin. You must be careful to do what has passed your lips, for you have voluntarily vowed to the LORD your God what you have promised with your mouth."*

Pastor, you made a vow to God to preach the Word and to be an example to the brethren. Let Paul's words to Timothy wash over you:

"I charge you in the presence of God and of Christ Jesus, who is to judge the living and the dead, and by his appearing and his kingdom: preach the word; be ready in season and out of season; reprove, rebuke and exhort, with complete patience and teaching. For the time is coming when people will not endure sound teaching, but having itching ears they will accumulate for themselves teachers to suit their own passions, and will turn away from listening to the truth and wander off into myths. As for you, always be sober minded, enduring suffering, do the work of an evangelist, fulfill your ministry" (2 Timothy 4:1-5).

The time has come, pastor, when people aren't putting up with sound doctrine anymore (2 Timothy 4:3). Our society definitely has turned their ears away from the truth and turned to myths. But your call is to *"always be sober minded, enduring suffering, do the work of an evangelist, fulfill your ministry."*

Do not allow society to dictate truth to the church, you are God's mouthpiece to speak truth to the world. Turn from keeping the traditions of your church to preaching the truth of God's Word. God's Word says, *"you nullify the word of God for the sake of your tradition which you are handing down"* (Mark 7:13 NIV).

E. M. Bounds, *"In true preaching, the sermon proceeds out of the man. It is part of him, flowing out of his life."*[1]

While preaching the Word is essential to the growth and sanctification of the church, I am convinced that the three most important things we need to be teaching our churches are:

- how to pray
- how to serve
- how to lead

In a broader sense, we must teach our people how to *learn, love* and *lead*; for we grow in our sanctification in all three.

Clear the Stage

Jimmy Needham recorded a song that for the past few years has left me a wreck for the modern day church. (I encourage you to find it and listen to it.) A portion of the lyrics follow:

Clear the stage and set the sound and lights ablaze
If that's the measure you must take to crush the idols
Jerk the pews & all the decorations, too

Until the congregations few, then have revival
Tell your friends that this is where the party ends
Until you're broken for your sins, you can't be social
Then seek the Lord & wait for what He has in store
And know that great is your reward so just be hopeful

'Cause you can sing all you want to
Yes, you can sing all you want to
You can sing all you want to
And still get it wrong [2]

It is not for me to attempt to exegete the lyrics of a song, however, I will close with this challenge, doubting many if any will accept the challenge, but here it is; perhaps you can adapt a modified version for yourself and for your church.

Clear the schedule of your church's calendar of everything but Sunday morning worship and a weekly prayer meeting for one year.

- No children's or youth programs
- No Sunday school
- No VBS
- No revival meetings or banquets

For one year. Just worship, study, pray, and observe The

Lord's Supper together every week, and see what God can do.

Pastoral Passion:

Pastor, you are the shepherd of the flock. The sanctification of the church as you care for your God appointed flock is your primary responsibility. Resist the temptation to follow the crowd in cool, hip, new thinking, and press into God in holiness.

When we think of modern-day pastors, here are some of the words that we are hearing to describe them: *Authentic, cool, contemporary, culturally relevant, innovative, intentional, millennial, missional, relevant, real.*

Now contrast that list to these attributes: *biblical, faithful, godly, holy, humble, sacrificial…called*!

We know God's desire is for us to be biblically applicable instead of culturally appropriate.

Far too many pastors are far too concerned with the administrative duties of the church, rather than the sanctifying duties of the church.

I am old enough to remember when society was shaped

by these three things: the press, the print and the pulpit, or, media, magazines and ministry. Now it seems the church has lost her influence, and she seems to be fine with surrendering the way of society to itself.

The Bride of Christ must be actively waiting for His return; she must be purposefully attempting to shape the society in which she exists, not merely drifting along for the ride, being blown here and there by cultural winds (see Ephesians 4:11-16). The church has become much too reactive rather than proactive.

We must not only know the Word of God; we must know the God of the Word.

The story is told of a Chinese Christian who visited the United States and toured churches here. At the end of the trip he was asked what he thought about American spirituality. He answered, *"I am amazed at how much the church in America can accomplish without the Holy Spirit."*

Any good coach would counsel his struggling team to get back to the basics. Any good pastor would lead their hungry, dumb, blind sheep to feast on prayer, the only virtue in which the early disciples asked Jesus for instruction.

What sinks most pastor's passion is thinking they have to make incredibly large changes all at once; then get disappointed and end up right where they were before – *dejected*, *discouraged*, *distraught* and *demoralized*. Taking a small step with specific goals may be all you need to begin to turn the ship.

One Indian chief once said, "Big ship. Long time turning."

Do not expect overnight success. Be patient. Do not get discouraged. It may take time to turn the ship, but it can be done.

Consider the drastic change in words when only one letter is changed:

Landfill – landfall;
Dull – Duel;
Ball – Bawl;
Scare – Scarf;
Deer – Dear;
Bare – Bear

Your life can have new meaning with simple, deliberate changes. Your life can be more effective if you will exercise your faith. Imagine what would happen to the church you lead if they had a new pastor, that is, a new you!

The Abel Label

Abel was a shepherd. Abel was the first death as well as the first murder. Abel offered the first born of his flock to God; Cain did not, therefore God did not bless Cain, so Cain killed Abel. Abel did not speak a single word that is recorded in the Bible, yet he was the first human to ever develop faith. Abel was the fourth human ever to live and yet the first that God thought was redeemable. Speak little, but let faith be your premiere attribute.

"We know that while we are at home in the body we are away from the Lord, for we walk by faith, not by sight" (2 Corinthians 5:6-7).

"If you dwell on your own feelings about things rather than dwelling on the faithfulness, the love, and the mercy of God, then you're likely to have a terrible, horrible, no good, very bad day. Our feelings are very fleeting and ephemeral, aren't they? We can't depend on them for five minutes at a time. But dwelling on the love, faithfulness, and mercy of God is always safe." – Elisabeth Elliot

Do not dwell on your feelings, they will have you like a

roller coaster, feelings will fail you. Dwell instead in your faith and allow God to ignite your passions once again. He will, if you will allow Him to. All He needs is a broken, humble servant, willing to seek Him at all costs.

You have a race to run, run it with integrity until you reach the finish line. No matter what you've done or how far you've gone, commit to get back in the race and run strong to the finish line. It seems so long ago now that Steve Farrar wrote his book simply titled, "Finish Strong." In that book, Farrar says, *"It is the rare man who finishes strong. It is the exceptional man who finishes strong. It is the teachable man who finishes strong."* [3]

What kind of label to you wish to have? You can have a say in that decision. If I must bear a label, let it be that I sought to know Jesus making Him known by allowing Him to sanctify me daily through the baptism of His Spirit and the reading of His Word with intimacy in prayer. Amen.

I suppose every artist struggles with when to drop the brush and declare the art complete. While there may be more I could add, at this point, I must declare this book done and put down the pen.

It will be my prayer that this work has served as an encouragement to you, helping to draw your attention back to your first love, Jesus, and your greatest calling, to preach the Word.

Perhaps someday I shall hear your story and share in your suffering as well as your joy, as it is made complete in us all by our Maker and King. I pray that God will complete in you what He has begun, and you will become a masterpiece reflective of the work of our Master and great Artist, Jesus Christ.

Run the race with perseverance. Finish strong!

THE AUTHOR

Keith is a gifted speaker, author, musician, worship leader and pastor. He and his wife Rana have been married over 36 years and have two daughters and five granddaughters. Keith enjoys speaking at retreats and conferences, and he and Rana have led several marriage conferences and retreats. Having had a conversion to Christ experience when he was 15-years-old, Keith is passionate about ministry and salvation of the lost, as well as discipleship and spiritual growth of believers. Keith and Rana currently live, work and worship in North Alabama where they own and operate a successful business and lead a thriving church.

Notes

Introduction

[1] www.statista.com

[2] https://newsroom.intel.com/editorials/intel-bong-chime-jingle-sound-mark-history/#gs.y1zf39

[3] Richard W. Dortch, *Losing It All and Finding Yourself*, (Green Forest, AZ, New Leaf Press, Inc. 1998), p. 8

[4] Ephesians 4:31

[5] 1 Timothy 6:12

[6] *Psychology Today* blog August 3, 2015. (https://www.psychologytoday.com/us/blog/understanding-the-erotic-code/201508/how-couples-can-survive-cheating-and-why-they-even-try)

Chapter 1

[7] https://www.mlive.com/news/grand-rapids/2013/04/ionia_chief_judge_fines_himsel.html

[8] John Eldredge, *The Utter Relief of Holiness,* (New York, Boston, Nashville, Faith Words), p. 118

[9] Dietrich Bonhoeffer, *The Cost of Discipleship*, first published in 1937 by Chr. Kaiser Verlag Munchen by R. H. Fuller, with some revision by Irmgard Booth; Copyright © 1959 by SCM Press LTD., First Touchstone Edition, 1995.

[10] Mike Courtney, *Failure and How I Achieved It*, © 2006 by Mike Courtney, p. 21-22

[11] Charles Haddon Spurgeon, *Lessons From The Apostle Paul's Prayers*, (Columbia, SC, Cross-Points Books), p. 14

[12] Matthew Henry, *A Commentary on the Whole Bible*, Fleming H. Revell Company, Old Tappin, NJ, Volume 6, p. 555

[13] 1 Corinthians 15:31

[14] 2 Corinthians 10:5

[15] John 14:16-17

[16] Max Lucado, *In the Grip of Grace: You Can't Fall Beyond His Love,* (Nashville, Thomas Nelson, 1996)

Chapter 2
[1] Song lyrics, *Revolution*, Songwriters: John Lennon / Paul McCartney, © Sony/ATV Music Publishing LLC
[1] Genesis 3:6 NIV
[2] 2 Samuel 11:2-3
[3] Bill Perkins, *When Good Men Are Tempted*, (Grand Rapids, MI, Zondervan 1997, 2007), p.32-33

Chapter 5
[1] Song lyrics, *Stubborn (Psalm 151)*, Songwriters: Brett James / Don Schlitz © BMG Rights Management US, LLC, Reservoir Media Management Inc
[2] 1 Peter 5:8
[3] Bill Perkins, *When Good Men Are Tempted*, (Grand Rapids, MI, Zondervan 1997, 2007), p. 49.
[4] 1 Peter 5:8 NIV
[5] John 8:44
[6] Clay Werner, *On The Brink, Grace for the Burned-Out Pastor*, (Phillipsburg, NJ, P&R Publishing, 2014), p. 82
[7] Rich Mullins album *Winds of Heaven, Stuff of Earth*, © Reunion, 1988

Chapter 6
[8] Richard W. Dortch, *Losing It All and Finding Yourself*, (Green Forest, AZ, New Leaf Press, Inc. 1998), p.35
[9] Numbers 32:23 NIV

Chapter 7
[1] W. J. Deane and S. T. Taylor-Taswell, "Proverbs," in The Pulpit Commentary, ed. by H. D. M. Spence and J. S. Exell (reprint, Grand Rapids: Eerdmans, 1983) 9:441
[2] Michael Hyatt & Daniel Harkavy, *Living Forward, A Proven Plan to Stop Drifting and Get the Life You Want,* (Grand Rapids, MI, Baker Books, 2016), p. 43

Chapter 9
[1] Matthew Henry, *A Commentary on the Whole Bible*, Fleming

H. Revell Company, Old Tappin, NJ, Volume 6, p. 370
[2] Richard W. Dortch, *Losing It All and Finding Yourself*, (Green Forest, AZ, New Leaf Press, Inc. 1998), p. 25
[3] IBID, p. 29
[4] Thriving on Chaos, p. 630, 1988
[5] Richard W. Dortch, *Losing It All and Finding Yourself*, (Green Forest, AZ, New Leaf Press, Inc. 1998), p. 43, 44
[6] Jim Cymbala, *Fresh Wind, Fresh Fire*, (Grand Rapids, MI, Zondervan Publishing House, 1997), p. 27
[7] IBID, p. 28
[8] Lyle Wesley Dorsett, *E. M. Bounds, Man of Prayer*, (Grand Rapids, MI, Zondervan, 1991), p. 134

Chapter 10
[1] Rick Warren, *The Purpose Driven Life*, (Grand Rapids, MI, Zondervan 2002), p. 17

Chapter 11
[1] John Eldredge, *The Utter Relief of Holiness,* (New York, Boston, Nashville, Faith Words), p. 126-7
[2] Richard W. Dortch, *Losing It All and Finding Yourself*, (Green Forest, AZ, New Leaf Press, Inc. 1998), p. 27
[3] The Cathedral Quartet, A Reunion, 1995.

Chapter 12
[1] Richard W. Dortch, *Losing It All and Finding Yourself*, (Green Forest, AZ, New Leaf Press, Inc. 1998), p. 10
[2] IBID, p. 10
[3] Mark Batterson, *Double Blessing, How to Get It. How to Give It.* (Multnomah, an imprint of Random House, 2019), p. 14

Conclusion
[1] E. M. Bounds, *Powerful and Prayerful Pulpits*, (Grand Rapids, MI, Baker, 1993), p. 55
[2] *Clear The Stage* lyrics © 2012, Simple Tense Songs, Ross King Music, Songwriters: King Ross Sullivan
[3] Steve Farrar, Finish Strong, (Multnomah Books, 1995), p. 8